TRAINING THE SAMURAI MIND

Also by Thomas Cleary

Alchemists, Mediums, and Magicians

The Art of War

The Book of Five Rings

The Counsels of Cormac

The Essential Confucius

Thunder in the Sky

Vitality, Energy, Spirit

The Way of the World

Zen Lessons

TRAINING THE SAMURAI MIND

A BUSHIDO SOURCEBOOK

Translated and Edited by Thomas Cleary

SHAMBHALA
Boston & London · 2009

SHAMBHALA PUBLICATIONS, INC.
Horticultural Hall
300 Massachusetts Avenue
Boston, Massachusetts 02115
www.shambhala.com

13 12 11 10 9 8 7 6 5

Printed in the United States of America

⊗This edition is printed on acid-free paper that meets the American
National Standards Institute Z39.48 Standard.
♻This book is printed on 100% postconsumer recycled paper.
For more information please visit www.shambhala.com.
Distributed in the United States by Penguin Random House LLC
and in Canada by Random House of Canada Ltd

The Library of Congress catalogues the hardcover edition
of this book as follows:
Training the samurai mind: a bushido sourcebook / edited by Thomas Cleary.
p. cm.
ISBN 978-1-59030-572-0 (hardcover: alk. paper)
ISBN 978-1-59030-721-2 (paperback: alk. paper)
1. Bushido. 2. Samurai—Conduct of life. I. Cleary, Thomas F., 1949–
BJ971.B8T73 2008
170'.440952—dc22
2007041865

CONTENTS

TRAINING THE SAMURAI MIND

INTRODUCTION

The caste and culture of the professional warriors of traditional Japan, best known to the West by the term *samurai*, developed over many centuries of historical change, ultimately to seize and sustain the position of dominant paradigm in Japanese society for seven hundred years. The culture of the samurai, incorporating elements of Taoism, Confucianism, Buddhism, and Shinto, along with the martial arts and military science essential to their original profession, came to be referred to as budo, the warrior's way; or shido, the knight's way; and finally bushido, the way of the warrior-knight.

Military culture has an ancient history in Japan, albeit one told in different terms according to the tradition of the telling. The imperial Shinto version, while relating to the earliest strata of Japanese legend and history, is the latest theme to emerge as a central feature in bushido ideology. While Shinto had by this time been influenced by centuries of contact with various elements of Confucianism, Buddhism, and Taoism, the militarized imperial Shinto revival in bushido began in some sense by attacking these very traditions.

Confucianism, originally associated with the establishment of a centralized state on the Chinese model, was reintroduced in new forms by Zen Buddhists in the thirteenth century, patronized by newly ascendant warrior chiefs. Emerging as an independent intellectual movement in the late sixteenth century, Confucianism was promoted by Japanese warlords as a means of civilizing the samurai. In one sense, this meant to prepare educated military personnel for peacetime administration of civil affairs as masters of the land. *Civilization* in the Confucian sense also meant to induce professional warriors to internalize a structure of subordination, including subordination of self-interest to public interest, in order to sustain social order and obviate perpetual power struggles among men at arms.

Taoism has had a more diffuse history in Japan than the other main intellectual imports, Confucianism and Buddhism, never having been institutionalized in any comparable way. It is probable, nonetheless, that the sort of Taoism ostensibly associated with the quest for immortality reached Japan by the end of the third century B.C.E., with sea expeditions sent eastward by the First Emperor of China, or with refugees from the same emperor's regime, or perhaps with both categories of people.

Other elements of ancient Taoism, practices commonly called magical or shamanic, seem to have entered Japan earlier, from both China and Korea. Taoist shamanism seems to have merged with its Shinto counterparts in Japan, particularly after being legally banned in the eighth century. Shamanic Taoism of the so-called Left-Hand Path, a sinister appellation also applied to an element of Tantric Buddhism, includes methods of demonic or magical warfare, brandishing destructive techniques based on mental or physical poisoning. This left-hand path, amalgamated with Shinto and Buddhist analogues, underlay the evolution of the lore of the *ninja* assassin. Events of ambiguous reality emerging from this tradition often mirror tactical use of insidious suggestion to cast enemies into states of mental terror.

INTRODUCTION

Taoist political philosophy and psychology appear to have entered Japan later than the shamanic and immortalist elements, being brought along with the massive importation of Chinese literature and technology into Japan beginning in the seventh century. For the purposes of bushido theorists, both in combat and in administration, the political, economic, and psychological theories of Taoism were essentially embodied in techniques of command and control, military tactics, and martial arts. Many of the most prominent samurai military scientists were steeped in Taoist-influenced Chinese strategic classics such as Sun Wu's *The Art of War*.

As the modern era approached and the sense of being surrounded by hostile powers spurred the development of a distinctly Shinto brand of bushido, some military thinkers in Japan began to repudiate the Taoist model of responsive action versus aggressive initiative, advocating the latter as more characteristic of the real history of Japanese warfare and more practical for Japan's true situation, as they saw it, in the international context. In tactical terms, the international military operations of the nineteenth and twentieth centuries under imperial command drew heavily on this latter Shinto conception of a native Japanese way of war.

Various techniques of both individual and mass combat advocated by more classical-minded bushido military thinkers of premodern times are informed by Taoist principles reflecting a general Taoist strategy of minimalism and essentialism. Another expression of this strategy that was incorporated into bushido is the samurai ethos of austerity. In both civil and military roles, austerity is often emphasized in bushido as an economic strategy for home and state as well as a mode of tempering and training the individual warrior.

3

This sort of pragmatic minimalism forms an element of Taoist political philosophy as well as a martial custom of perpetual preparedness. In addition, Buddhist asceticism and its less radical Confucian counterpart also played an important role in the rationalization of the austerity of bushido, particularly after the end of endemic warfare and the establishment of national peace and order in the seventeenth century eliminated immediate consciousness of the need for austerity on the part of the ruling warlords and their knights.

Like Taoism, if later in time, Buddhism originally entered Japan with immigrants from China and Korea. Buddhism was eventually to become a political factor in the sixth century, when emblematic artifacts were sent to the Japanese court by the king of Paekche on the Korean peninsula. As it happened, the implications of this diplomatic mission in terms of international trade, military alliance, and domestic political patronage precipitated a conflict between powerful Japanese clan factions. This dispute ultimately resulted in the vanquishing and dissolution of the redoubtable Mononobe military clan, a historical ally of the imperial clan with intrinsically Shinto roots, who opposed the adoption of Buddhism at the imperial court.

Buddhism was ultimately established as a sort of state religion by the first historical Japanese constitution of 604, attributed to the celebrated Prince Shotoku. The second article of this famous document says, "Earnestly respect the Three Treasures. The Three Treasures are Buddha, Dharma, and Sangha. These are the ultimate refuge for all forms of life, the supreme religion of myriad nations. Who in what era has not valued this teaching? People are rarely very bad, and can be taught to follow it. If they do not take refuge in the Three Treasures, by what means can the crooked be straightened?"

This declaration seems to value Buddhism for both domestic

and international purposes, seeing in it a source of moral reconstruction as well as a medium of membership in a well-established transnational culture and community. Other articles of the constitution combine elements typically associated with Confucianism, Taoism, and Legalism in China, exhibiting an early and influential manifestation of syncretism, a recurring practice in Japanese religion also seen in some strains of bushido.

Over the centuries succeeding the acceptance of Buddhism as an official religion in Japan, major Buddhist institutions acquired large estates dedicated to their support. The Japanese Buddhist world became in effect an alter nation, with its own internal pseudostates, including sectarian armies. A system of ecclesiastic titles was constructed to mirror the structure of the imperial government, and Buddhist studies were conceived in a quasi-Confucian fashion as a vehicle for obtaining rank.

The secular mind-set with which elements of institutional Buddhism became imbued under these conditions is complained of as a living reality by the famous Zen master Dogen six hundred years after Prince Shotoku:

> The mistake that has arisen among students here is that they consider the respect of others and the forthcoming of property and riches to be the manifestations of virtue; and other people also know that and think so too. Knowing in your heart that this is the affectation of the demons of temptation, you should be most deliberate. In the Teachings this is called the doing of demons. I have never heard, among the examples of the three countries [India, China, and Japan], that one should regard material wealth and the reverence of the ignorant as virtues of the Way. (*Shobogenzo-zuimonki*)

As the old order of imperial rule lost ground to the rising samurai, the sects supported by the aristocracy were also confronted with rivals to their religious monopolies. When the warrior class asserted independent sovereignty, and a separate central military government was established in the twelfth century, the dominant cultural force in Japan was in many respects Buddhism, but in this role it had largely been confined to the control of the old aristocracy. As some distinguished monks began to break away from the established sects to create or import new cults, while the samurai also asserted independence, the potency of Zen Buddhism in particular was recognized by the new military masters of Japan, both as a cultural base of political influence and a psychological training system for warriors. Many of the soldier-samurai of the lower orders, in contrast, were drawn to the emergent Pure Land sects of Buddhism that proposed eternal life after death for the faithful.

Although Buddhism is ostensibly the only one of the Japanese religious and philosophical traditions featuring an explicit prohibition of killing, this proscription was not considered applicable to soldier-monks in monastic armies envisioned as protectors of Buddhism, nor to samurai in their role as police and protectors of society and state. According to the seventeenth-century Zen master Bankei,

> Although there is killing such as the striking down of enemies in advance of the ruler, to destroy evil people to keep order in the world is the normal task of samurai, so such acts are not called murder on the part of samurai. Only when they contrive to kill for personal reasons, due to their own conceits, motivated by selfish desires, does it become murder.
> (*Bankei Zenji Hogo*)

Nonetheless, whatever the license allowed to samurai in this respect, the emphasis on compassion found within Buddhism was in time harshly rejected by some bushido writers, claiming that Buddhism made men soft and therefore should not be part of the samurai education, training, or belief. On the other hand, generations of patronage and symbiosis with the samurai caste had a hardening influence on institutionalized Zen, as lamented by Daien, an eighteenth-century master of Bankei's lineage:

> Nowadays Zen monasteries all over gather crowds of three to five hundred; minutely regulating every moment, they fetter their bodies so it's like going to prison. Anyone who commits even the slightest infraction is beaten and expelled, never forgiven at all. The invasive surveillance and cruelty in monasteries are worse than those of the police. For this reason, when a retreat is over, some are sick and some are disabled. This is killing off youth before they mature, creating hatred of teachers and parents. (*Shogan Kokushi Istujijo*)

It may be that this institutional culture of violence was a response to growing criticism of Buddhism as decadent, soft, and parasitical. Records of some circles also indicate habitual infliction of mental and physical violence on disciples unrelated to regulatory infractions but, rather, represented as a part of Zen training itself. Nonetheless, however adapted to samurai culture Zen may have been, and however fashionable retirement into Buddhist orders may have become among the upper echelons, according to sectarian histories very few professional warriors ever really attained Zen enlightenment. Historically speaking, therefore, the greatest contribution of Zen Buddhism to the development of bushido and samurai culture may have been the introduction and promotion of neo-Confucianism.

Neo-Confucianism was largely a product of Song dynasty China, when it was a norm for secular scholars and government officers to study with Chan (Zen) masters. In this way both Taoism and Confucianism became infused with certain elements of Buddhist practice, resulting in the development of distinct new schools of neo-Taoism and neo-Confucianism. While neo-Taoism gained comparatively little currency in Japan, neo-Confucianism was more amenable to the purposes of the samurai ruling class: austere like Zen but offering social and political dogma suitable to rationalization of rulership.

Zen monasteries remained key repositories of neo-Confucian learning for hundreds of years, but by the sixteenth century some Zen scholar-monks began renouncing their Buddhist vows to become professional Confucians. The erroneous yet widespread belief that Zen is nihilistic had in fact created its own organs of self-confirmation, as the critical literature complains, and the renunciation of Buddhist orders for secular scholarship reflected a sociopolitical consciousness disaffected with what was perceived as a demimonde of artificial alienation and irresponsibility created by the cloister.

The institutionalization of neo-Confucian studies by Shogun Tokugawa Ieyasu in the seventeenth century subsequently dominated the educational systems of Japan and made this type of thought standard for more than two hundred years. This move consolidated a policy initiated in the sixteenth century by one of Ieyasu's predecessors, the warlord Oda Nobunaga, who razed thousands of monasteries to reduce the political influence of Buddhism and promulgated a code of law explicitly designating Confucianism as the proper curriculum for warriors and ministers of state.

In many cases, as a result, the voice of Confucianism outweighs or displaces the voice of Buddhism in the expression of bushido. Even in the local *terakoya,* temple primary schools operated by Buddhist monks, the curriculum was Confucian. The popular *kana-hogo,* or vernacular sermons, of Zen masters of the Tokugawa era are heavily larded with Confucian concepts, sometimes by way of conventional contextualization, sometimes transformed into metaphors for psychological self-government.

In this way Buddhist doctrines and practices were also absorbed into secular Confucian studies, contributing a characteristic creativity and independence of spirit to secular scholarship. In spite of the official espousal of one particular school of neo-Confucianism, some scholars soon began to reject this limitation to rediscover and reinvent a wider spectrum of Confucian thought and practice, even at considerable personal risk to themselves.

While religious Shinto was influenced by Buddhism and state Shinto by Confucianism, a new Shinto nationalism rejecting Chinese traditions began to emerge in the seventeenth century. Although there were some crypto-Buddhist precursors to nationalism in the thirteenth century, particularly in the Nichiren sect and the so-called School of the Time, a version of Pure Land Buddhism, nationalism did not ferment into its modern form until the nineteenth century, when a mood of xenophobia pervaded certain samurai minds. The primitive concept of *blood* indoctrinating and animating the psyche and culture of Nazi Germany in the twentieth century can also be found in a Japanese form in nineteenth-century Shinto-style bushido:

> The term *uji* [clan] means *u-ji,* "birth blood." The term *suji* [lineage] means *su-ji* "pure blood." The term *Michi* [Way, or Path] compares the nation's roads to

the blood vessels in the human body, clearly meaning *mi-chi* "true blood." This national character esteeming the bloodline was an auspicious custom with clear divisions, but long ago it got so that lords and subjects intermingled, different castes intermarried, so bloodlines became illegitimate. (Banbayashi Kohei, 1813–1864, *Omoidegusa*)

Both Buddhism and Christianity were stigmatized as *foreign* religions in this process of fabricating the modern myth of pure blood:

When the false cultists of the West came here, they used arts of deception to delude the minds of the people, plotting to change the Land of the Kami (Shinto deities) into a territory of wily barbarians. Then when Oda Nobunaga killed off the evil monks throughout the provinces, from Mount Tendai on down, he perceived the treacherous plot of the West and moved to expel the false cultists. Toyotomi Hideyoshi banished the false cultists beyond the sea. (Aizawa Seishisai, 1782–1863, *Taishoku Kanwa*)

In terms of its historical rationalization of imperial rule, Shinto-oriented bushido is concerned with establishing the central position of the ancient Yamato conquest, with emphasis on the role of the emperor, empress, or crown prince as the undisputed commander in chief of the armed forces.

The realities of ancient Japanese history are complex and controversial, even today leading the investigator directly onto a battlefield of cultural and political combat, particularly concerning relationships among territories that were to become parts of what are now called Japan and Korea. An original impetus of the ideological warfare waged by Shinto-based bushido was to reinterpret history so as to elevate Japan above both Korea and China, both militarily and culturally, laying the psychological foundation for the rise of imperial Japan in modern times. Thus the roots of this trend in bushido writings can be seen as early as the seventeenth century, while acute escalation of mythic might is marked in the nineteenth century, on the eve of confrontation with Western powers.

A number of clan or guild organizations are traditionally associated with the establishment and expansion of the Yamato state, the precursor of imperial Japan, particularly the *Otomo, Kumebe, Mononobe, Saekibe,* and *Hayato.* Although some of them became clan names and surnames, they appear to have originated as professional organizations. The *Otomo,* or "major retinue," is frequently mentioned, portrayed as an elite corps of warriors in the personal service of the emperor and also commanders of the *Kumebe,* or "organized groups," on the frontiers.

The *Mononobe* organization is often mentioned along with the *Otomo.* The term *Mononobe* was anciently used as a general word for government functionaries but came to be especially associated with state security duties, such as keepers of arms for the *Otomo,* town police, prison guards, and eventually warriors and garrison soldiers. The *Mononobe* are depicted as geographically distributed in twenty-five or eighty clans, depending on the source, suggestive of an occupying force consistent with their reputation of having assisted the *Otomo* in establishing a new center of Yamato sovereignty on the main island of Japan in antiquity.

This prehistoric conquest is one of the most important scenarios of Shinto-based bushido doctrine. It has been suggested, nonetheless, that the original *Mononobe* may have been earlier inhabitants of the island submitting to and allying with forces moving in from the southern island of Kyushu.

The other two ancient military organizations, the *Saekibe*, or "assistant chiefs," and *Hayato*, short for *Hayabito*, or "swift men," were composed of captives seized from other peoples already inhabiting the land. The original *Saekibe* were Ainu from the north and east of the main island, modern Honshu, while the original *Hayato* were Kumaso, thought to be of Malay ancestry, who inhabited the southern island, modern Kyushu. The captive *Saekibe* were redistributed outside the perimeters of the new imperial territory, in the manner of garrison guards like the *Mononobe*, while the vanquished *Hayato* warriors seem to have been used for armed retinues analogous to the *Otomo*. In ancient times the *Hayato* were associated with both magical and material warfare, considered experts in casting curses.

Eventually the head of the *Saekibe* was executed and the organization was dissolved on charges of dereliction of duty. The same thing happened to the *Otomo* army. The *Hayato* were not merely disbanded but destroyed, murdered en masse when their loyalty and tractability became suspect. The *Mononobe* were dissolved when their leader opposed the powerful Soga clan over the political issues associated with the importation of Buddhism in the sixth century.

While various circumstantial reasons are thus traditionally given for the disappearance of the old military orders, there may have been an underlying impetus for these changes in the overall attempt of the imperial Yamato government to establish an unchallenged unified state with a monopoly of power. Given the strength of the clan system and the physical barriers to communication presented by the terrain, this was a challenging endeavor. After a major administrative reform in 646, as the imperial establishment actively adapted Chinese models in this state-building effort, the military was reorganized to assert and support a centralized civil command.

With the concentration of wealth and expansion of urban culture consequent upon the assertion of central power and the importation of Chinese technology, clan leaders were increasingly drawn from their provinces to the capital city. While these aristocrats peopled the central government, the internal administration of their rural domains in matters such as tax collection, security, and criminal justice were delegated to men of lesser status. Customs of polygamy and primogeniture generally ensured a supply of such men in aristocratic houses.

Over time, this class of men evolved into the warrior caste commonly known as the samurai. The word *samurai* originally meant "attendant," referring to the armed retinues of aristocrats. When they became an independent class, the samurai referred to themselves in more dignified terms as *bushi*, warrior-knights. As land managers, security chiefs, and provincial governors for their upper-class relatives, these samurai came to acquire enough power on their own account to redefine their relationships with the central administration. Ultimately the concept of an overarching military authority emerged among leading samurai clans.

Like the ancient imperial ideal, the idea of a comprehensive military command was never completely implemented until the middle of the nineteenth century, when civil and military command were reunited by the Meiji Restoration. Nonetheless, in the attempt to assert a supreme martial authority, three successive samurai governments dominated the stage of Japanese history for many hundreds of years.

The martial element of the founding myth of the imperial clan, and the process of division of civil and military authority in the course of Japanese history resulting in the rise of the warrior caste, are represented in a summary fashion in an imperial proclamation to the armed forces in 1882 as part of the ideological preparation of the new national military for a campaign of international conquest:

> Our nation's military forces have been led by the emperor generation after generation. It has been twenty-five hundred years since Emperor Jimmu personally led the warriors of the Otomo and Mononobe in ancient times to strike and subdue those of the central realms that had not submitted, so he could assume the throne and rule the land.
>
> Since then, as the state of society changed, the military system also changed repeatedly. In antiquity, the official system was that the emperor personally led the armed forces. Although the empress or the crown prince sometimes substituted, generally speaking military authority was not entrusted to ministers or subordinates.
>
> Coming to the middle ages, civil and military systems were both modeled after those of Tang dynasty China (618–907). Six departments of guards were established, left and right stables were set up, and security personnel were posted, so the military system was well ordered.
>
> Becoming accustomed to continuing peace, however, court administration gradually shifted to cultured weakness, so soldiers and farmers spontaneously split into two, and at some point the conscript soldier of old turned into a warrior, and then eventually into a knight. Military authority devolved entirely upon the leaders of those knights, and as society fell into chaos, the main power of government also fell into their

hands, becoming a military government for about seven hundred years.

Even though there is nothing that human effort could have done to reverse the social changes leading to this condition, nevertheless, being inimical to our nation's body and contrary to our ancestral system, it was a deplorable state of affairs.

This rhetoric reflects some long-standing social issues as well as some relatively new problems. The association of peace and cultural pursuits with military weakness had been a specific concern of bushido theorists ever since the pacification of Japan under the Tokugawa regime in the seventeenth century. For the political and economic purposes of the samurai rulers, tales of the decadence of the old Japanese aristocracy and the indulgences of Chinese emperors and kings were employed to justify permanent martial government, even in peacetime, by asserting the moral and pragmatic superiority of the austerity of the warrior's way. This was confirmed, in their eyes, by the ignominious demise of the great Ming dynasty of China at the hands of Manchu mercenaries in the 1640s.

The downfall of native government in China and the increasing presence of Europeans in Asia provided major motivations for the political unification of Japan as well as for the policy of excluding foreigners instituted by the Tokugawa regime in the seventeenth century. Perceived as threatening to Japan, European activities also intensified the argument that peace makes people weak, as military scientists of later generations increasingly complained that the prolonged Pax Tokugawa had made the samurai soft and negligent, requiring remedial revivification of martial culture if Japan were not to fall prey one day to alien interests.

The literature of bushido is immense, expressing many different views and voices. The various elements of the cultural and historical background within which bushido evolved—Buddhism, Confucianism, Shinto, Taoism, Legalism, military science, and martial arts—were selectively combined in various proportions by different thinkers, producing a wide range of diverse attitudes and ideas about human nature, society and government, compromise and conflict, peace and war, and the future of the known world. This volume presents selections from the many voices of bushido, translated from the works of twenty-two writers, ranging from the fifteenth to the nineteenth centuries.

[ONE]

SHIBA YOSHIMASA (1349–1410)

Shiba Yoshimasa was originally a member of the Minamoto, which had been the clan of the first shogunate (1185–1338), generally known after its location in Kamakura. Shiba also used the surname Ashikaga, of the ruling clan of the second Shogunate, centered in Muromachi, Kyoto. Son of a provincial protector (shugo, or military governor), Shiba Yoshimasa served several stints as governor general (kanryo) under Ashikaga Yoshimitsu, led military campaigns against rebellions, and was Protector of several provinces. Eventually he retired into Buddhist orders.

In the essays translated here, Shiba combines Buddhist, Shinto, and Confucian concepts and practices in discussing the moral and psychological development of the warrior. In connection with religion, he is critical of institutionalized, formalistic observances from both economic and spiritual points of view. Having seen action himself in warfare, Shiba was clearly conscious of the difference between ceremonial display and inner fortitude. He refers to religious and moral concepts as tools for cultivation of courage, character, and intelligence, opposing all sorts of hypocrisy and artifice, including the popular practice of praying for resolution of personal problems, which he viewed as creating a sense of weakness and dependency. He also applies a critical caveat to the ideal of self-sacrifice, in a sense the supreme sacrament of bushido, insisting that a moral context is necessary to validate a warrior's death.

■ ■ ■

One should be objective and perceptive in regard to all things. These days there are few people who are that discriminating or determined.

17

Wielders of bow and arrow should behave in a manner considerate not only of their own honor, of course, but also of the honor of their descendants. They should not bring on eternal disgrace by solicitude for their limited lives.

That being said, nevertheless to regard your one and only life as like dust or ashes and die when you shouldn't is to acquire a worthless reputation. A genuine motive would be, for example, to give up your life for the sake of the sole sovereign, or serving under the commander of the military in a time of need; these would convey an exalted name to children and descendants. Something like a strategy of the moment, whether good or bad, cannot raise the family reputation much.

Warriors should never be thoughtless or absentminded but handle all things with forethought. This is also what Watanabe no Tsuna taught to Urabe no Suetake, to master the ultimate crisis beforehand.

Most people say you should act according to the time, in view of the moment, but when there is big trouble they get excessively flustered. Sneaking past the proper time to die, they regret it afterward.

It is said that good warriors and good Buddhists are similarly circumspect. Whatever the matter, it is vexing for the mind not to be calm. Putting others' minds at ease too is something found only in the considerate.

People's character and inner hearts are evident in the way they invariably behave, so even when nobody's there to see you, think of the walls as eyes and don't let down your guard. In your manners among other people, needless to say, you should not make a single misstep. Even in saying a single word you shouldn't give others an impression of being shallow. Even if you are only a lover of beauty with flowers on your mind, keep your mind graceful and sincere, enjoying sensual pleasures on that basis.

Even in man-woman relations, without genuineness there is no earnest sensuality, but at least there's rarely heartbreak.

————

When you begin to think of yourself, you'll get irritated at your parents' concern and defy their instructions. Even if your parents may be stupid, if you obey their instructions, at least you won't be violating the principle of nature. What is more, eighty to ninety percent of the time what parents say makes sense for their children. It builds up in oneself to become obvious. The words of our parents we defied in irritation long ago are all essential. You should emulate even a bad parent rather than a good stranger; that's how a family culture is transmitted and comes to be known as a person's legacy.

————

As human beings everyone should know that we ought to revere and honor the buddhas and deities, so there's no need to restate this; but there's something here that is to be understood. Whether it be the emergence of buddhas in the world or the manifestations of deities, in any case it is for the sake of society, for the sake of human beings. So it doesn't mean condemning people. It is so that people may purify their minds, properly practice humaneness, justice, courtesy, intelligence, and faith, and understand fundamentals. Apart from that, why should buddhas and deities appear?

While ignorant of this basic motive, on the premise of believing in Buddha they trouble the populace, taking things from people to build temples and cloisters. On the pretext of revering the deities they just round people up and perform shrine ceremonies. This way, it seems to me, must be contrary to the service of both buddhas and spirits.

Even if one doesn't perform any religious exercises and never makes a visit to a shrine, neither deities nor buddhas will disregard a person whose mind is honest and compassionate. In particular, the Great Goddess of Ise, the great bodhisattva Hachiman, and the deity of Kitano will dwell in the heads of people whose minds are honest, clean, and good.

Also, people only pray at shrines and so forth when they've got personal troubles. That seems quite vain. You shouldn't pray to buddhas or deities for anything but a good state in the afterlife. That's what will be effective; yet even that, it has been taught, doesn't get directly to the true path.

————

People all think that serving the ruler is a matter of offering up your personal loyalty and public service according to the favors you receive first. This is a backward understanding. Being able to live in the world is due to the benevolence of the ruler to begin with. Forgetting that fact, people set their sights ever higher and come to resent society and the ruler too. This is very worrisome.

————

When people in society who should be in civil service demean themselves, thinking it won't be easy for them, this is a regrettably foolish thing. Having been born a human, you should aspire to surpass the masses and help other people, making it your pleasure to do your utmost for others, lifetime after lifetime, generation after generation. Since this alone is the purpose of the bodhisattva, if while an ordinary person your aspiration is equivalent to that of a bodhisattva, what satisfaction could be greater than that?

————

People with wisdom and intelligence are perceptive in employing others. It is a typical habit to use someone for everything if you think he's good. When you employ a warrior for a civil role, or make an ineffective speaker into an ambassador, or use a dull man where intellect is needed, the person's whole life can be wasted because of the mismatch.

People should be employed in roles where you can see they're suited. If the curved are made into wheels while the straight are made into axles, there will be no useless people. Even someone you don't like may well be useful for something; and even if you like someone, what good is that if he is useless to you?

People without sincerity of heart should not be considered for anything. It seems to me that this is the sort of thing referred to by the expression that all abilities come from one mind. For warriors in particular, if you calm your own mind and discern the inner minds of others, that may be called the foremost art of war.

For a person to be bad tempered is more disgraceful than anything. No matter how irritated you may be, at the very first thought you should calm your mind and distinguish right and wrong. If you are in the right, then you may get angry.

When you get angry unreasonably, on account of your own bias, people won't be intimidated, so even if you get madder it's no use. People should only be intimidated and ashamed at truth, so when something is merely annoying you should take care to calm down and rethink the matter. It is a good thing to be willing to change when you're wrong. It is most problematic to insist on thinking and behaving in a certain way, regardless of good or bad, just because that's what you've been doing.

Then again, if you suppose that goodness means keeping quiet like a three-year-old child, and you can't even get angry, letting things go when they should be resented, lamented, or made a lesson for others, getting to be known to people as someone who goes along with whatever others may say or do, that is bad for others and will be a loss for you. It is better to criticize what should be criticized, even while keeping your mind at ease, saying what needs to be said, and not be considered an ignorant, mindless person.

Personalities like that could be called good or bad in ancient times, when people were particularly good. These days, they just play upon others, or simply seek to fool them, so those who are always gentle and graceful are regarded with contempt. When Buddhists, as so-called mindless wayfarers, seem to have no eyes and no mind, or seem like little children, that is a different matter. And ignorant people who don't know when something's wrong and just stay silent should not be called good people. This much you should carefully consider and distinguish.

Those who practice sitting meditation, such as monks, are bright in all affairs even if they're not sharp by birth, because they quiet their minds. Scholars too, regarding their work as the most important thing, quiet their minds to learn, so they are spontaneously sharp in other things too.

However, the human mind can become good or bad, keen or dull, depending on how it's used. A person's prime is no more than ten years; during that interval, one should enjoy everything. From the age of ten to fourteen or fifteen there's no real true enthusiasm for things, and by the time you're forty or fifty your mind becomes dull and generally sluggish, so you can't develop any new skills in a satisfactory manner.

Since you've only got from eighteen or nineteen to about thirty, you only have twelve or thirteen years to accomplish something and acquire a source of satisfaction. In this unstable world, we should be quick to learn.

While we are living in the human world, usually not one thing out of ten conforms to our wishes. Even a sovereign ruler can't live as he wishes. That being the case, if we in our present condition try to impose our will somehow on things that do not accord with our wishes, ultimately we must submit to the discipline of the order of nature.

No one would think they'll be vindicated today since they were mortified yesterday, or that they'll succeed in their aims this year because they were unsuccessful last year. Continuing a mind that is like dust, even as though nonexistent, from moment to moment, more and more, the person acting should forget about wishes. For resentment to remain, you must be a twisted person.

The term *twisted person* is condemnatory by both social and religious standards. For anyone to become egotistical and obstinate and refuse to forget is shortsighted and weak. Yet if you try to clear your mind deliberately, that is creating extraneous thought.

Take care to base everything on people, and not to deceive. When it comes to combat, even if you're a youth you should keep your spirits up and think there's no one stronger than you. Think you'll be a source of strength for others, and think them reliable too.

You should never inquire about matters concerning warfare from someone born timid, no matter how well you know him.

You shouldn't try to avoid the work of the moment just because it's dangerous. You shouldn't prosecute an illegitimate war just because it's easy.

Generally speaking, when combat is bound to be easy, you let the other side make the first move. When it's going to be dangerous, you should consider it your task alone, even if it takes a hundred tries.

Deceptive behavior is especially bad in combat.

[TWO]

ICHIJO KANEYOSHI (1402–1481)

A descendant of the powerful Fujiwara clan, of which the Ichijo were an offshoot, Kaneyoshi served as regent (sessho), a post he soon resigned, and was twice chief adviser to the emperor (kampaku). An expert in Shinto and Buddhism as well as Confucianism, he ultimately retired into Buddhist orders.

The admonitions translated here were written for Shogun Ashikaga Yoshinao (r. 1473–1489). In accord with the religious temper of his time, Ichijo weaves concepts of authority, power, and responsibility into a prayer to Hachiman, the Shinto god of war envisioned as a Buddhist protector of Confucian justice. He tends to apply Buddhist values such as honesty and universality to modify the mental restrictions ordinarily imposed on attitudes by clannish customs and hierarchical organization; as advice to a ruler, the ideals of clarity and compassion are devoted to facilitating good government.

■ ■ ■

Pray to the Great Bodhisattva Hachiman

As long as you have the job of shogun, this prayer is a form of national defense. The commission to govern the sixty-six provinces of Japan may be a result of past conduct in former lives, but it is due to your parents, your father and mother. If you do not govern the land to restore an orderly society, there will be no point in occupying that office.

25

"May my authority be increased by the grace of the great bodhisattva Hachiman"—when you pray for power this way, it is not so that you might do as you wish yourself. Over the last ten years or so, samurai families as well as noble houses, even monastics and laymen and laywomen, have been deprived of their land, on which their lives depend; having seen their distress and suffering, overwhelmed with pity, you therefore look to the divine will, determined that you would rectify matters if only you had the power.

The point is that if the governors of the provinces don't truly reform their thinking, behave peacefully and amicably, and act with kindness and compassion, they should be struck all at once with divine punishment. If we return to an orderly society, your aspiration in the present lifetime will be fulfilled, and you'll be known to posterity as a great shogun. There can be no better way of being remembered in society, but it must be possible for the great bodhisattva. Every morning, wash your hands, rinse your mouth, face south, and pray with utmost sincerity. If the deity actually exists, why wouldn't he accept your prayer?

If this intention of yours is not hidden from the world, those who learn of it will either fear the divine will or be shamed by martial dignity, so the mentalities of the governors will change, and you can easily make this a civilized, united land.

Filial Conduct Should Be Primary

No one, high or low, has no parents. The significance of our debt to our parents is expounded in both Buddhist and Confucian classics. Buddhist teaching says we couldn't repay this debt even if we carried our parents around the polar mountain every day on our shoulders. Confucian teaching says we have received our bodies, hair and skin, from our parents, so not daring to injure them is the beginning of respect for parents.

For example, as someone's offspring, since one's body is entrusted by one's parents, to be careful of one's body and behave in such a way that one suffers no wound or infirmity would be a way of filial conduct. The reason is that parents grieve and sorrow when their children are ill or injured, so if you take care of your body you don't grieve your parents; therefore this is filial conduct.

Next, when parents make mistakes, if their children don't remonstrate, that too violates filial duty. When they are mistaken, you should admonish them without hurting their feelings, speaking softly without showing anger. If that is ineffective, then it is filial conduct to admonish them so that they change their attitude even if you have to convince them by weeping, or pretend to become angry.

If you are not filial to your parents, as a result your own children won't be filial to you. You'll realize it when the time comes. Although the habits of ordinary people are such that they cannot behave as beautifully as it says in scripture and classics, nevertheless everyone should understand the principles.

Honesty Should Be Valued

Buddhist teaching speaks of being straightforward, dropping expedients. The revelation of the great bodhisattva Hachiman also says that the spirit resides in an honest head.

Honesty just means a straightforward mind. If the mind is distorted, all behavior is distorted.

In dealing with people, recognize good people as good and reward them; recognize bad people as bad and punish them. This is straightforward government practiced with a straightforward mind.

A straightforward mind is like nothing so much as a mirror. If a fine-looking person looks in a mirror, it reflects a fine appearance; when an ugly person looks in the mirror, it reflects an ugly appearance. This is why a Buddha's knowledge is called universal impartial mirroring knowledge, likening it to a mirror. The true character of a deity can also be depicted as a mirror.

Kindness and Compassion Should Be Wholehearted

Kindness means the wish to relieve suffering; compassion means the wish to give happiness. In a Buddha's heart is the thought of relieving suffering for all beings and giving them happiness. This is the meaning of kindness and compassion.

In Confucian classics this is called humaneness. Humaneness means the attitude of love toward humanity. The word may be different, but the meaning is none other than kindness and compassion.

Even birds and animals, when trained and domesticated, arouse feelings of sympathy; how much the more so human beings! To exercise sympathy for them all is surely the conduct of a humane ruler.

In these last ten years or so, countless millions of people of all classes, high and low, have been separated from their homes and oppressed by hunger and cold. The perpetrators of unjust confiscation and plunder like this act as they do because they are devoid of kindness and compassion. Their failure to realize they'll suffer the consequences of their actions is despicable.

Practice Arts

The arts of archery and horsemanship are of course your family business, so they need not be mentioned. Besides these, you should follow your preferences in poetry, kick ball, and other hobbies. The third Ashikaga shogun used to attend imperial parties and even had a taste for music and song. Taking things that far is a superabundance of refinement. Whatever it is, something that can please your company ought to be cultivated, according to the time.

Even cheers on drinking wine, as an act accompanying enjoyment, should be offered to everyone. What details could there be? However, even in the discourses of Confucius it is written that wine alone has no specific measure, except not to become disorderly. It depends on whether or not one is a drinker, with no other rule, so it is said there is no specific measure. Not becoming disorderly means you shouldn't become intoxicated to the point of losing your basic nature. When you have enjoyed it to the point where your spirits are high and you think you're drunk, it's best for everyone to retire early, for a lot of misdeeds may occur. If your familiars get drunk and sloppy, don't say anything while they're still drunk, but after they've sobered up ask them if they remember how they behaved and warn them to be more circumspect in the future—that would be extremely supportive.

Keep Government in Mind

Whatever I say, what it boils down to is simply that there's nothing like just administration of government. In recent years, those who have forcibly taken over the lands of monasteries and shrines are led by viciousness, apparently unconcerned about their reputation in future generations. Although they are from families that have been loyal and ethical in public service for generations, suddenly they disgrace the legacy of their ancestors. This is unspeakable. Whatever happens in their own lifetime,

29

if they don't have the sense to think of their posterity they are being extremely inconsiderate, are they not?

For this reason, under no circumstances should matters of government be neglected. Regarding people who do not respond to the decisions of the managers of the noble houses, it appears reasonable not to hear their representations. When you relax your mind in respect to the general or the particular, then no distinction will be made between the blameworthy and the blameless. Furthermore, if you take up matters you've already dismissed, people with all sorts of ambitions will come forth. This should never happen. Once you've already made a definitive judgment, if you're asked for authoritative instruction in a matter that a magistrate could easily decide, what's the use? In cases involving one party, just stamp the information files, relying on the official findings. When two parties are suing each other, even in cases of violation of monastic rules, have them judged by two or three people—anyone will do—and it should be quite easy to find who's in the right.

If something has been misheard or overlooked, when a retrial is held, whatever is to be corrected is not something new but must have been there from before.

Since administration involves myriad affairs, even a day or two of neglect will not do. Ignoring them altogether would be a travesty.

THREE

NAKAE TOJU (1608–1648)

Nakae Toju's paternal grandfather was a samurai in the service of a feudal lord, but his father was a farmer. He became his grandfather's ward while still a boy, after the death of his father. He began to study Confucian classics when he was ten, but the region where he lived was rustic and there were no teachers. When an itinerant monk from Kyoto began to lecture on Confucius, Toju was the only one who attended, and the monk left after a few days. According to all accounts, the local culture was strictly martial, and samurai there despised literary studies, so Toju studied alone and in secret.

Nakae Toju wrote his first book, an exposition of the Confucian Great Learning, when he was twenty-one. He was in the employ of a feudal lord in Shikoku for a time, but he left because he could neither induce his widowed mother to relocate there nor obtain permission from his lord to return home to look after his mother. This is a classical Confucian conflict of conscience, which may well have been a cover for an unspoken issue with the lord or his administration that could not be safely specified.

Resolving to leave in secret, Nakae sold all of his household belongings to acquire a quantity of rice equivalent to his salary for a year. Then he left it in the house when he departed, indicating his intention to return his salary to his lord. Vowing never to serve another lord, he subsequently refused all offers of employment and made local education his life's work. While his short life was thus spent in humble circumstances, he is well respected and well loved for his dedication to education.

With no source of income, Toju took up small-time commerce and lending in addition to teaching. It is said that his loans were always repaid without fail because his interest was low and he never pressed people for payment.

In 1640 Nakae Toju discovered the works of Wang Yangming (1472–1529), a Ming-dynasty neo-Confucian of great renown, a civil and military leader as well as an original thinker, whose work virtually reshaped Confucianism. Toju became converted to Wang's way of thought, and historians consider him the founder of Wang Yangming Studies in Japan.

This school values practical virtue over academics, and numerous stories are told of Nakae Toju's embodiment of this teaching. He died when he was only forty, and little of his work is preserved, some of it having been destroyed by his own hands after his conversion. He is said to have made a powerful impact on the manners and mores of his locality by virtue of his character and personality.

Nakae emphasizes the inseparability of cultural and martial training, his ideal of warriorhood devoted to protection and preservation of the civilizing influence of culture. In this he compares culture and warriorhood to embodiment of the cardinal Confucian virtues of humanity and justice. Characteristically, his approach emphasizes the inner reality of personal development, devoting attention to both the form and spirit of education, training, and behavior.

Nakae also writes at some length about military science, again distinguishing fundamentals and derivatives, concentrating on purpose to inform procedure. Here the psychological condition of the successful warrior emerges as a prime concern in connection with political and social purposes of warfare. This interest in the human effects of conflict is especially marked in Taoism, and as Nakae proceeds from consideration of military training to the rule of law in civil administration, his views in this domain also exhibit a distinct Taoist element.

■ ■ ■

It is said that culture and warriorhood are like the two wheels of a chariot, or the two wings of a bird. Are culture and warriorhood distinct? What do culture and warriorhood refer to?

Common convention seriously misconstrues culture and warriorhood. Common convention takes culture to mean reading poetry, writing verse, mastering calligraphy, and having a soft, refined personality; while warriorhood is taken to mean learning shooting, riding, and arts of war and military science, and having a fierce and stern personality. Both are approximate but inaccurate.

Fundamentally culture and warriorhood are a unified character, not separate things. Just as the creative force of the universe is one energy distinguished into yin and yang, the sensitivity and efficacy of human nature are a single quality with distinctions of cultural and martial. Culture without warriorhood is not true culture; warriorhood without culture is not true warriorhood.

Just as yin is the root of yang, and yang is the root of yin, culture is the root of warriorhood, and warriorhood is the root of culture. With heaven as the warp and earth as the woof, governing the nation and keeping social relations in order is called culture. When there are perverse and unprincipled people who obstruct the course of culture without fear of divine order, to bring them to punishment, or raise an army to attack them and unify the government of the whole land, is called warriorhood.

So it is that the ideograph for *warrior* is composed of a combination of two characters meaning "weapon" and "stop." Since warriorhood is in the service of culture, the root of the warrior's war is culture. Since culture is for governing with the threat of armed action, the root of culture is warriorhood.

Culture and warriorhood are inseparable from everything else as well. To properly practice the principles of respect for parents, brotherliness, loyalty, and faithfulness is called culture. To strive to subdue whoever obstructs respect for parents, brotherliness, loyalty, and faithfulness is warriorhood.

As an analogy, suppose there were only the sunny skies of spring and summer, without the shade of autumn and winter, or only the shade of autumn and winter without the sunny skies of spring and summer—the process of creation that produces myriad beings would not come to fruition. Just as the two energies of yin and yang are differentiated yet are fundamentally the circulation of one basic energy, culture and warriorhood are fundamentally one and the same enlightened quality. Warriorhood without culture is like the shade of autumn and winter without the sun of spring and summer, while culture without warriorhood is like the sun of spring and summer without the shade of autumn and winter.

Culture is a different name for the path of humaneness, warriorhood is a different name for the path of justice. Because humaneness and justice are a single virtue of human nature, culture and warriorhood are a single quality, not separate things.

Realizing the virtue of humaneness and justice, you should understand the conditions of culture and warriorhood. Culture that is contrary to humaneness may be called culture in name but is not culture in reality. Warriorhood that is contrary to justice may be called warriorhood in name but is not warriorhood in reality. If you do not develop an adequate appreciation of the true content of culture and warriorhood, your mind will be quite unclear, handicapping you greatly in all sorts of things.

Now then, in culture and warriorhood there are root and branch, namely virtue and art. Humaneness is the virtue of culture and the root of cultural arts. Literature, music, manners, writing, and mathematics, as arts, are outgrowths of the virtue of culture. Justice is the virtue of warriorhood, the root of martial arts; such things as military principles, shooting and riding, and methods of warfare, as arts, are the outgrowths of the virtue of warriorhood.

When you work on learning the fundamental root virtue first and practice the derivative arts second, uniting culture and warriorhood, comprehending both root and branch, you are a genuine cultured warrior, and a true Confucian.

Cultural arts without cultural virtue are no use to the process of culture. Martial arts without martial virtue are useless for the ways of warfare. It is like the way plants and trees cannot produce fruits without roots. To call a genteel personality and refined behavior culture, or to say that ferocity and severity should animate the activity of a warrior, is low-level, shortsighted vision.

There are people who appear to be soft, easygoing, and casual yet are spirited and animated in military action. This is called hidden courage. As I see people of the world who have performed successfully in combat, on the whole many of them are characterized by this hidden courage. On the other hand, there are people who appear to be as fierce and severe as demons but are exceptionally cowardly. This is likened to having the disposition of a sheep but the skin of a tiger.

A sheep is an animal so gentle it wouldn't even stomp a bug, while a tiger is a ferocious beast that will eat humans and other animals. If you put a tiger skin on a sheep, it may look ferocious, but since it's a sheep underneath, its behavior, unlike its appearance, is meek.

Although there are many more examples right before our eyes, it seems there are few people in the world with clear vision.

———

Does this mean cultural arts and martial arts are unnecessary?

No, that is a misunderstanding. The point is that it is unbalanced to seek to learn the outgrowths without the root. One who has mastered cultural and martial arts on the basis of fundamental humaneness and justice is a noble man of many talents who comprehends both root and branch. In common parlance this is someone with both flowers and fruit. Cultural and martial arts based on fundamentals are exceptionally valuable. They are essential to the sense of order of fundamentals and derivatives.

What about those who do not comprehend both fundamentals and derivatives—what should they do?

It's better to ignore the derivatives and learn the fundamentals. Since ancient times many people have been able to practice cultured ways without having cultural arts, or have achieved military successes without knowing martial arts. That was because they worked on the fundamentals first. This should be well understood.

If we say that there are a lot of people with hidden courage, would we say those who appear to be easygoing ought to be animated in military actions?

This is a shortsighted interpretation. To say that there are a lot of people with hidden courage means that you cannot tell just by a superficial view of appearances. There are surely cowards among those who appear easygoing, while there will also be courageous ones. There are also bound to be cowards among those who appear to be fierce, as well as those who are indeed mettlesome. The perceptivity to aim for is the ability to see whether someone is courageous or cowardly at heart.

They say there are two kinds of courage—the courage of humanity and justice, and the courage of bloodlust. What is the difference?

Noble men of enlightened character wish for nothing whatsoever but to preserve justice and reason and act in a principled way. As they are not distracted by desirousness, in establishing justice and reason, acting in a principled way, they are willing to sacrifice their lives for their lords and parents, so they have no fear of death or attachment to life. Because of this, they have nothing to fear between heaven and earth. Facing thousands and myriads of enemies, they are like tigers and wolves facing foxes and badgers, without fear. Having no fear, they are supremely brave. Because the humaneness of their enlightened character is clear, this courage naturally exists within humanity and justice, so it is called the courage of humanity and justice. Because it is such supreme courage that it has no rival in the world, it is also called great courage. True warriorhood is nothing but this great courage.

The courage of bloodlust makes no distinction between reason and force, justice and injustice. It is nothing but ferocity, overcoming others, and not being afraid of anything. Like the ferocity of tigers and wolves, therefore, it can perversely impede the human path. Being brave and having no fear resemble the courage of humanity and justice, but having no discrimination between reason and force, justice and injustice, merely inclined to bloodlust, the behavior of tigers and wolves is very lowly. The ones with status start rebellions, the poor ones become bandits.

What is more, the mind that fears on account of desire because of greediness is no different from the coward that fears death. Since those with the courage of bloodlust ultimately take desire to be fundamental, in a victorious army they may look good striving for martial valor and acting loyal and ethical, but over the ages many professional warriors have ignominiously abandoned their lords in defeat. This sort of thing is only the bravery of bloodlust. Because it is of no use to justice and reason, it is called the courage of bloodlust.

With only the bravery of bloodlust, there is tremendous risk in desire, so it is not useful for the Great Way uniting heaven, earth, and humanity. It is only useful for the bloodlust of the little body, so it is also called small courage.

———

Are there ways to use great courage and small courage?

There is nothing wrong with the use of great courage, and there is never a wrong time to use it. In all of your activities, in all of your social interactions, you cannot practice the Great Way without it. In the army, it's good for top commanders as well as lowly soldiers.

Men of small courage are only useful for service in military action. This may be good enough for a lowly soldier, but not for a top commander. Since ancient times, in both Japan and China, countless commanders of small courage have lost victories. This is something to beware of.

———

It is said that there are various practices and many systems of military science. Is this something a commander has to know?

Military science is something a commander has to know. A general who doesn't know military science is like a fletcher who doesn't know how to fletch.

To compare military science to the human body, humaneness is the heart; surveillance and espionage are the eyes; surprise and convention are the hands and feet; banner and pennant, cymbal and drum, the manufacture and employment of weaponry and equipment, scheduling and so on, are the skin and hair.

So in the understanding of most people, only the skin and hair are thought of as military science. That is why they say there are many systems. In terms of the manufacture of banners, pennants, cymbals, drums, weapons, and equipment, and matters of scheduling, every clan has its own organization, so there are lots of systems. Because these are only the skin and hair, it is impossible to say definitively which are good or bad; this must be considered and determined in context, depending on the time and place. Even innovations determined by the methods of a general without reference to traditional systems will do. It should be realized that there are many systems because it doesn't make that much difference in terms of victory and defeat.

Since surveillance and espionage and surprise and convention are the eyes and hands and feet of contention, they're the same practical science, which does not differ by school or system. If these eyes are clear and these hands and feet skilled, you succeed in winning one hundred percent of your battles, earning you the epithet of master general. If these eyes are clouded and these hands and feet incompetent, you always get your army beat; the commander gets his army beat by his bad command—this is called being a bad commander.

In this sense, if you interpret the skin and hair alone as military science, with no understanding of these eyes and hands and feet, that is the lowest of the low.

Diagrams of formations in military science originate from the *Book of Changes*; complete since the time of the Yellow Emperor, they have been handed on from age to age by savants such as Taigong and Zhuge. The Japanese vernacular translations abound with errors, so the texts should only be studied in the original. Just understanding the formation of diagrams of military science as they are is the same as learning to judge horses from pictures of scenes. Selecting something unsuitable in ignorance is likened to seeking a swift steed according to a picture.

In ancient times there was a famous general in China whose son read and studied his father's books, but he had no understanding of how to change according to the situation. After his father died the son became a general, but he suffered such massive defeat that he became a laughingstock of the nation. This

was because of simply studying the skin and hair without working on the eyes and hands and feet.

People who would study military science should first enter
the school of a true Confucian and clarify the enlightened virtue
combining the cultural and martial in one. Then after having
established this basis they should study the original texts of military science, making sure to focus on exercise of the eyes and
hands and feet. This is truly the most urgent task of warriors.

————

*There have been many famous generals in Japan and China since ancient times
who mastered military science and achieved military successes without learning Confucian psychology, so one would think it should be possible to learn
military science without the polish of psychology. Thus it may be unclear
as to why it is said that military science should be studied after mastering
Confucian psychology.*

This is an important issue. People born with the capacity to
be great generals may master military science and achieve military successes without the polish of psychology, but without
that quality of character they get deluded by their ability and
come to like killing. Since they act unjustly and immorally, the
populace sorrows, having been injured by their poison, so eventually they are visited by divine punishment, losing their lives,
while their nations perish too. The evidence for this is that in
both China and Japan there were very few generals who had
only physical power and lacked character yet who remained
unscathed and whose posterity flourished. This can be seen in
the histories and documents of Japan and China.

The basic motive of military science is national stability and
security, and perpetuation of military success, in order to benefit
the populace. If instead the populace is injured, one's own luck runs
out, and the state is ruined on this basis, then even mastery of military science and achievement of military success are ultimately use-

less mischief. If on top of that you concentrate only on scheming, relying on the power of deception without the virtues of humaneness and justice, even if you have tremendous talent you cannot even stand up to a disciplined enemy, much less an army of humanity and justice—that would be like a bug trying to stop a chariot.

In the *Book of the Shadow of the White Flag* it says that a skillful attack cannot match warlike soldiers, warlike soldiers cannot beat elite knights, elite knights cannot match a disciplined system, a disciplined system cannot oppose humanity and justice. The sense of this statement should be thoroughly savored.

It is for this reason that of Sun Tzu's Five Things, the Way is first, while in Wu Tzu's *Art of War*, harmony is first. Whether called the Way or harmony, in either case this refers to the virtues of humanity and justice. Since there's no way to clarify these virtues other than Confucian psychology, it is said we should learn military science after having worked on psychology and clarified those virtues. This is evident. In any case, if we are going to study military science, shouldn't we learn the military science of the humane who have no rivals on earth?

What about the legal system—should the laws be numerous and strict?

The individual items of a punitive system of laws are determined according to time and place, so whether it's better to have more or less cannot be determined dogmatically. Some matters should be dealt with strictly, moreover, and some are better treated leniently, so whether to be strict or lenient cannot be decided dogmatically either. It's best just to pursue the reasoning appropriate to the time, place, and situation.

Punitive law also has root and branch. The root of government is the enlightenment of the mind and ethical conduct of the ruler defined as the model and mirror for the whole country. The individual stipulations of the laws are the branches and leaves of government. Since the preferences of the ruler are imitated by everyone all the way down the hierarchy, when the ruler's mind is enlightened and he acts ethically, then people's minds become good naturally, even without laws. All the more so when both root and branches are authentically and aptly effected, the nation thrives and survives forever.

Governing by the branches alone without the root is called legalistic administration and is not wholesome. Legalistic administration always has an abundance of rules that are strict and severe. The penal system of the First Emperor of China was the epitome of legalistic administration. The stricter it is, the more legalistic administration breeds rebellion. The prime example of this can be seen in the era of the First Emperor.

Government including both root and branches is rooted in minimalist optimization of adaptability to the times. Governing the minds of people ignorant and deluded as they are at present is likened to clarifying cloudy water. The more you fiddle with it, the cloudier it gets. If you refrain from fiddling with it and let it settle, the pollutants naturally sink to the bottom and the water becomes clear from above.

The difference between government by character and government by law should be well understood. Government by character means first correcting your own mind and then correcting the minds of others. This is like the plumb line and square of the carpenter, which when in proper condition correct warping.

Government by law means trying to correct the minds of others without one's own mind being upright. As proverb says, the ruler should be the measure, plumb line, and compass; if the ruler's mind is enlightened and his judgments are correct, his laws are principled and therefore endure unaltered. If the ruler's mind is ignorant, then matters are not well considered, so his laws vary from occasion to occasion.

[FOUR]

SUZUKI SHOSAN (1579–1655)

Suzuki Shosan was a reputed Zen master, a veteran warrior turned Buddhist monk. As a samurai, he fought for Tokugawa Ieyasu in two campaigns, one when he was only twenty-one, the second when he was already thirty-five. Retiring from active military duty after Ieyasu had succeeded in establishing the Tokugawa Shogunate in the early seventeenth century, Suzuki later spearheaded yet another campaign, this time on the cultural front, writing a polemic against Christianity to bolster the Tokugawa ban on the religion, which was seen as a front for European invasion of Japan. His popular preaching nonetheless contains a great deal of supernatural threat and promise, unlike mainstream Zen Buddhism.

In his instructions specifically for samurai, Suzuki emphasized internal Zen psychology and focused on using the professional requirements of the samurai life as a framework for spiritual cultivation while also reinvesting spiritual development in the perfection of performance in the line of duty. Accordingly, whereas the importance of motivation by reward and punishment figures prominently in typical military and political treatises, Suzuki Shosan is one of the thinkers in bushido who explicitly disavowed the profit motive in professional performance.

■ ■ ■

Do your job with your mind as taut as an iron bow strung with wire. This is identical to Zen meditation.

43

Use your mind strongly even when you walk down the street, such that you wouldn't even blink if someone unexpectedly thrust a lance at your nose. All warriors should employ such a state of mind all the time in everyday life.

There is a practice designed to enter the Way of Buddha by means of your profession. You should apply this idea, that a man born in a house of valor, polishing a sword and sporting a bow, should always apply attention strongly, as if he were marching right into an army of ten million men.

The strongest men and the greatest masters of martial arts are born that way, so no effort can attain that; but when it comes to exerting our whole heart and disregarding our lives, to whom should we be inferior? No one should think he'll be beat, even by the greatest warriors. Why? Because if you back down to such a person, who will back down to you?

Thus you are always on duty, required to apply your full attention firmly. If you slack off, you're no use.

Be aware that this stable, firm attitude is itself meditation practice. There is no other method of concentration to seek. Even Buddhism itself is just a matter of applying full attention steadily, without being disturbed by things. Developing a confident attitude that is never pained or vexed or worried or saddened or altered or frightened is called attaining buddhahood.

There are those who discuss the amount of rewards and size of entitlement of men who have exercised considerable military valor, laid their lives on the line, ground down their bones, and become famous. They are foolish! Why not do a warrior's deed, costly though it be, for the sake of loyalty? People who think of rewards are nothing but military merchants.

There are myriad different methods of practice, but essentially they amount to no more than overcoming thoughts of yourself. The source of suffering is ego, the thought of self. To know this is reason. Knowing the reason for suffering, what a sense of duty does is evoke effort to extinguish the thought of self with a genuine courageous mind. People without reason don't understand the source of misery and happiness; people without a sense of duty cannot break the bonds of life and death.

Daily Activities of Warriors

A warrior asked, "They say the law of Buddha and the law of the world are like the two wheels of a chariot. But nothing would be lacking in the world even without Buddhism. Why liken them to two wheels of a chariot?"

Shosan replied, "The law of Buddha and the law of the world are not two separate things. According to a saying of Buddha, if you can enter the world successfully there is nothing more to leaving the world.

"Whether Buddhism or worldly law, there is nothing more than reasoning correctly, acting justly, and practicing honesty.

"There are differences in depth of honesty. Not twisting reason, preserving justice, correctness in social relations, not crossing people, not being egotistical—these constitute honesty in the worldly sense. This is a way into the deep via the shallow.

"Honesty in the context of Buddhism means realizing that all conditioned phenomena are illusions, and using the original reality-body in its natural state. This is true honesty.

"The fact is that the ordinary people are very sick patients, while the Buddha is a very great physician. Ordinary people ought to recognize sickness first. In the ignorant mind that fluctuates, there is the sickness of delusion, there are sicknesses of greed and false views, there are sicknesses of weakness and injustice. Based on the mind infected by the three poisons, there are diseases of eighty-four thousand afflictions. Getting rid of this mind is called Buddhism. How is this any different from worldly law?

"People who attain the Way know the principle of fundamental emptiness, use principle and duty as a forge to temper this mind day and night, get rid of the residue of impurities, make it a pure unhindered mind-sword, cut through the root of selfish and obsessive thoughts, overcome all thoughts, surmount everything, and are unfazed by anything, unborn and undying. These are called people of the Way.

"Now, then, ordinary people are those who take the falsehood of illusions to be true, produce a selfish mind attached to what has form, develop greedy, angry, and ignorant thoughts, create all sorts of afflictions and lose their basic mind, always distracted, overcome by thoughts as they occur, racking their brains and belaboring their bodies, without buoyancy of mind, vainly passing the time benighted, alienated from themselves and fixated on things. This is called the mind of ordinary people.

"That being so, you should know the different terms for the original mind. It is called the adamantine actuality, the indestructible body of reality. This mind is not hung up on things; it is unafraid, unshakable, undismayed, unfazed, undisturbed, and unchanged, master of all. Those who realize this and use it effectively are called great; they are said to have iron guts, and to have attained the Way. People like this are not obstructed by myriad thoughts; able to let go of all things, they are very independent.

"However, people who would practice the Way of Buddha will be unable to succeed unless they have an intrepid mind first. It is impossible to gain access to the Way of Buddha with a weak mind. If you are not rigorously observant and do not practice vigorously, you will experience misery along with those afflictions.

"One who overcomes all things with a firm mind is called a wayfarer. One who has thoughts fixated on appearances, is burdened by everything, and so suffers misery is called an ordinary person.

"So people who work up the courage of violence with an afflicted mind may have the force to break through iron walls for the moment, but violence eventually comes to an end. The mind of a strong person, being immovable, does not change. If men who are warriors cultivate this, why would they not attain a strong mind?

"Even in the case of people of outstanding heroism, when the killing demon of impermanence comes, their usual power comes to an end, they lose their ferocity, and they cannot exert any effort. When they try to open their eyes they cannot see anything; their ears are faint, their tongues shrivel, and they cannot speak. When the killing demon enters the heart and destroys the internal organs, breathing becomes labored, pain permeates their bodies, and with its force they show timidity toward the killing demon of impermanence, unable to bear the great hardships of death mountain, drowning in the river between here and the afterlife, shamed at the court of the king of death, falling forever into the three evils and four dispositions, disgraced generation to generation, lifetime after lifetime, as self and as other, unable to escape. Would you say this disgrace is insignificant because people of superficial society don't know of it? Disgrace even in illusory human society is nothing to take lightly; how much the more so eternal disgrace!

"Can someone ignorant of this logic be called someone who knows principle or embodies justice? So you should think ahead.

If you know the principle, you should fear it. If you embody justice, use the fierce and firm mind-sword to cut down the enemy of birth and death and live in great peace."

Question: The way to practice Buddhism is consummated in knowing principle, practicing justice, and realizing the importance of honesty. Please give more detailed indications of how to practice honesty.

Answer: Although the paths of cultivation have a thousand differences and myriad distinctions, what is essential is no more than quelling selfish thought. The source of suffering is self, the thought of self. People without reason do not discern the source of misery and happiness; people without justice cannot cut the tie of birth and death. Give a hard look.

So in the mind of ordinary people, there are buoyant attitudes that overcome things, and depressive attitudes overcome by things. To act with a buoyant attitude is the doorway into the realm of buddhas; to act with a depressive attitude is the roadway into hell. With the power of the vow dedicated to liberation, you should keep a buoyant attitude day and night.

Here are types of buoyant attitudes, substantiated by bravery:

1. An attitude of constant vigilance over birth and death
2. An attitude of gratitude
3. An attitude of unhesitating advance
4. An attitude acknowledging the principle of cause and effect
5. An attitude of observing the inconstancy of illusion
6. An attitude of observing the impurity of this body
7. An attitude of being careful of time
8. An attitude of faith in the Three Treasures
9. An attitude of self-sacrifice for your leader

10. An attitude of watching over yourself
11. An attitude of self-sacrifice
12. An attitude of acknowledging your own errors
13. An attitude like being in the presence of nobles or rulers
14. An attitude of commitment to benevolence and justice
15. An attitude of attentiveness to the words of buddhas and Zen masters
16. An attitude of compassion and honesty
17. An attitude of consideration of the conditions of the most important matter

These attitudes emerge from the brave and resolute mind, so they are free of attachment of any sort, beyond things, and therefore buoyant. Even if you die in action, you won't suffer much.

People who would cultivate these attitudes should only set their eyes on images of such figures as Vajrasattvas or the Immovable One. These represent the attitude of overcoming devils. If you have a brave and resolute heart, you should know this. Don't gaze on them with a faint heart.

When this brave heart is continuous, the citadel of mind is secure and you have unobstructed independent moral force. Even if an army of demons eighty-four thousand strong arises at once and attacks you, they cannot even face you—instead, they lose their power, are drained of strength, and will all disappear.

If people specialize in martial valor, why would they not exercise this attitude? If you are weak-minded, with thoughts fixating on things, the army of demons will gain strength, increase in power, and immediately invade the citadel of your real essence and confound your mind-king; the six bandits will perk up in delight, deviant devils will gain freedom and fly through the eighteen realms, eventually landing you in hell. You have to be prepared!

Here are types of depressive attitudes burdened by things:

1. A negligent attitude forgetful of self and careless of mind
2. A tourist's attitude living on hiking in the mountains
3. An attitude ignorant of justice and reason
4. An attitude ignorant of the principle of cause and effect
5. An attitude ignorant of the vanity of the evanescent
6. An attitude of interest in fame and fortune
7. An attitude of ostentation
8. A suspicious attitude
9. An obsessive attitude
10. A weak and cowardly attitude
11. A greedy and callous attitude
12. A judgmental attitude
13. An egotistical, arrogant attitude
14. An attitude of jealousy in love
15. An ungrateful attitude
16. An obsequious attitude
17. An attitude oblivious of birth and death

Also, there are seven feelings—joy, anger, sorrow, care, pity, fear, and surprise. It is said that myriad illnesses derive from these seven feelings. Attitudes like these are states of mind that come from darkness and are of limitless variety, but they can be diagnosed by means of the foregoing presentation.

Because they emerge as embodiments of obsession, as they occur from thought to thought, as you are overcome by those thoughts and lose the original mind, these are states of mind sunk in pain and torment.

When you dwell in these depressive states of mind, if duty suddenly requires you to die, your distress will be intense. So to overcome oneself is considered sagacity, while to suffer under the burden of one's own mental state is considered stupidity.

When you manage to overcome your own mind, you overcome myriad concerns, rise above all things, and are free. When you are overcome by your own mind, you are burdened by myriad concerns, subordinate to things, unable to rise above.

"Mind your mind, guard it resolutely. Since it is the mind that confuses the mind, don't let your mind give in to your mind." This song is superlative. When you indulge your mind, thoughts fixated on appearances increase and you fall into the three mires [of greed, aggression, and folly]. When you slay your mind you arrive at buddhahood immediately.

An old saying goes, "Kill, kill! If you stop killing for a moment, you'll go to hell like an arrow shot." Pay attention to sayings like this. *The Scripture on Mindfulness of Truth* says, "The wise are always sorrowful, as if confined in prison, the ignorant are always happy, as if they were in heaven." The buddhas speak like this. The focus of past sages should not be unfamiliar. You should know what is most important. Why should you wind up in hell by enjoying this body, a dream phantom?

You have to correct your mind time and again. If our personal state of mind shows in our faces, it will be hard to interact with people.

Just strengthen your conscience, abide by the principle of honesty, develop the power of the vow to detach from appearances and detach from names, let go of everything, relinquish your life with the brave energetic power of faith, and proceed intently and urgently on the unexcelled Way.

When this attitude is uninterrupted day or night, resolution permeating your being, kept up even in dreams, so that it ultimately matures, inside and outside will naturally become one, and all of a sudden you'll wake up from the past dream, and Buddhism and worldly laws will both be realized, spanning past, present, and future, extending throughout the ten directions.

[FIVE]

KUMAZAWA BANZAN (1619–1691)

Kumazawa Banzan was taken to the capital city of Edo at the age of seven, subsequently taken into the service of a feudal lord at the age of fifteen, and assigned an annual salary of seven hundred koku of rice (one koku = 5.119 U.S. bushels). Some years later he resigned, considering himself too young and immature. He became a student of Nakae Toju, with whom he studied Wang Yangming Confucianism for more than a year. He returned to the service of his former lord when he was twenty-seven, this time with a salary of only three hundred koku.

Rising rapidly in the ranks, eventually Kumazawa was given charge of the administration of the entire domain, now with a salary of three thousand koku. Expanding agriculture and promoting education, he advocated a system of assistance that proved effective in sustaining the populace through a flood in 1654 and a famine in 1655. He had levees constructed and irrigation channels dug for the public benefit.

In 1656 Kumazawa was injured while hunting and retired from public service. Going to Kyoto, he studied classical music and Shinto mythology while also lecturing and writing. With his fame growing, he was victimized by slanderers and went into hiding. In 1669 he was hired by another lord, in whose employ he remained for more than ten years, through two territorial transfers, a disruptive method by which the Shoguns exerted control over regional lords. In 1685, already in his late sixties, he was put under house arrest by command of the Shogunate, which had taken offense at one of his writings, and he eventually died in the castle where he'd been confined for years.

Kumazawa's writing addresses a wide range of concerns. Dealing with the requirements of leadership and warriorhood, he distinguishes the products of natural capacity and formal training in both martial and cultural dimensions, emphasizing the accurate assessment of individual potential in order to employ people with maximum efficiency. He also insists on the interposition of moral reasoning and common sense between the attitude of the warrior and the element of personal prestige in the external motivation structure of samurai society.

Consistent with his concept of social service as the foundation of warrior culture, Kumazawa was one of the first to point out the flaws in the economic system, whose ill effects he already perceived in spite of growing general prosperity. The closure of the country to foreign trade, however, and the closure of the Confucian mind to social mobility handicapped understanding of the structural impasse of the economic system of late-feudal Japan.

Nevertheless, Kumazawa's ideas on economics and politics are not without historical precedent or visionary perspicacity. Seeing both urbanized samurai and land-bound farmers unnaturally vulnerable to fluctuations in the grain market because of the need to convert rice into currency, like ancient legalists and future socialists, Kumazawa advocated central government control of large-scale commerce to prevent the operation of the monetary system from creating poverty in the midst of prosperity.

■ ■ ■

Warriors who have mastered martial arts may know how to beat people, yet there are those among them with no military achievements. On the other hand, there are many who have military achievements even without martial arts, and there have been military professionals who were killed by civilians.

The same goes for scholarship. Intelligence, humaneness, and courage are cultural and martial virtues; manners, music, archery, horsemanship, writing, and mathematics are cultural and martial arts. People who are by nature humane and warm are respectful and loyal even without education; people who are by nature brave and strong have an advantage in battle even if they don't know martial arts.

But that doesn't mean there is any reason to abandon cultural or martial arts. Even if people couldn't carry out the Way completely themselves, the ancients would educate them with literary skills, giving them a broad liberal education so they could liberate the people from superstitions and improve customs. Even people of little courage, if they had the talent for martial arts, were trained in archery and horsemanship and were taught all military methods, to strengthen the people, make them polish their skills, and fortify the martial presence of the nation. This is how rulers and generals maximize their advantages by not discarding anyone.

———

Warriors who are illiterate and have no understanding of philosophy should at least be devoted to the warrior's way first and foremost, determined to elevate their reputation without fail if something should happen at any minute, considering it a matter for regret to die in bed of illness.

Even so, it is a mistake to think this way capriciously. If you wish to elevate your reputation, others also have the same idea. Death or life—it's one or the other. Even if it doesn't come to that, if there's trouble involving bows and arrows and guns, the chances of dying are ten times the chances of surviving. If you hope for some incident to occur so you can elevate your reputation and establish yourself, that's ill-considered.

If you think you'll elevate your reputation by the luck of victory, without realizing that the chances of dying are ten times the chances of living, you may likely lose out when you see the trend of events going unfavorably. On top of that, considering the sorrow and suffering of the wives and children of men all over the land, even if you're sure to survive and enhance your reputation greatly, are you glad to cause myriad people to suffer for one person's puny salary, accumulating people's lamentation in exchange for fame and profit?

For a humane man, even if he wins a nation, or the whole world, it is not something he desires. A military text says, "Normally an army does not attack cities that have done no wrong, and does not kill innocent people. To kill people, take their territory, and use their money and goods is called robbery."

To wish there to be bad people and want disorder to erupt so that you can elevate your reputation is disloyalty. What is more, there are fluctuations in wealth and nobility, poverty and lowliness, flourishing and decline; to be averse to armed rebellion with this understanding is the proper attitude. Without this understanding, even disliking the way of the warrior and martial arts, to like peace and security just for the convenience of soft living, though different in kind, would be equivalent to someone capriciously hoping for an incident to occur.

A good warrior is always courageous and deeply devoted to the way of the warrior and martial arts; he takes care not to stumble no matter what happens, respects his ruler, pities everyone from his wife and children to the old and young all over the world, and prefers peace in the world from a humane and loving heart. If, on top of that, there are men who forget themselves and their homes and perform great feats when unexpected emergencies arise, achieving military success, even if illiterate, they are knights of the paths of both culture and arms.

The convention of referring to those who know both cultural and martial arts as knights of both paths is not the ultimate. These accomplishments should be referred to as cultural and literary *arts*—the arts alone, absent the virtues of intelligence, humaneness, and courage, cannot be called *paths*.

———

They say hidden courage is the best courage, but even a sword with a fine blade may be found to fail when tested. It seems that the relative strength of people's martial courage is also like this. Of course, there must be such a thing as hidden courage, but some say it seems to be in but one of a hundred men, whereas most are no different than they appear.

Whether a sword will cut or not can indeed be seen from the blade. In olden times the warriors rarely had tryouts, so it is said that they used to choose swords with good blades just by judging them with their own eyes. If we focus on learning that, we too are generally correct in our assessment. A blade that is well tempered and shines as if it had a soul is one that will cut. A blade that is hard yet spiritless and stony may appear to be tempered but is weak, dull, and won't cut. Once you've come to notice these good and bad qualities, they become apparent.

There are also blades that are generally inscrutable. There are some that seem dull but are not, whose keenness and fine temper are invisible, like the sky clouded over, or like the depths of a deep pool. These are exceptional weapons. Hidden courage is like this too.

All warriors are logically supposed to have martial courage; all swords can cut. The grip and scabbard of a sword are decorated with gold and silver threads, and it is sheathed appropriately, neither too soon nor too late. Since warriorhood in principle is supposed to be embellished with culture, it is good for courage to be encased in humaneness, by being polite, humane, and loving in everyday life. Being quick with your swords is not actually a natural function; personal mishap is near at hand. As long as your bravery is like quickness with a short sword, you should sheathe it properly.

What is more, those who boast of their valor and strength often get hurt. If you try to claim your goodness you lose it, and if you boast of your skills you lose them. This is an ancient maxim. One who makes a show of valor is hated by others, so even if he achieves something it is not praised but denied. They say, "Why is he contriving to stand out—even with exceptional merit it is hard to attain a great estate." So he always has lots of enemies and no peace of mind.

In the old days there was a man who made helmet and armor his pillow and mountain and meadow his house for thirty years, who not only distinguished himself time and again but also was accomplished in the affairs of the warrior's way. When the younger fellows got together they'd invite this old man and listen to stories of the warrior's way. That man said, "I don't have as much merit as people say. Ever since youth I was loving and respectful, and so I have been liked by others. This is why I have a lofty reputation in the world. The ultimate meaning of warriorhood is love and respect."

Whatever the occupation, when you get to the ultimate, that is near the Way.

———

It is said that those who are cheerful and willful are not good on the battle line. It is also said that those who are cunning in regard to gain and loss are slow in combat. One might wonder whether there is a way to perceive strength and weakness.

It is said that it may be assumed that men who are simply direct by nature are generally good in combat. It is also said that combat is normal for warriors, like tilling for the farmer. Warriors consider it best to be mannerly, just, and reasonable in everyday life. They should not be given big salaries and made heads of others solely on account of action in combat.

As it is *under a distinguished commander* that *there are no weak soldiers*, you shouldn't assume that samurai are generally good in combat. Even the cheerful and willful are not born cowards; they have just unconsciously gotten into the habit of being that way. If they act capriciously toward someone who is direct by nature, it is an aberration and thus is not tolerated. Then, running into something they hadn't expected, they make a miserable showing.

Also, those who make a show of astuteness and have a lot of interests don't set their minds on justice and reason all the time, so they are called cowards because they lack justice and reason when these are natural.

When yin climaxes it gives birth to yang, and when yang climaxes it gives birth to yin. So when it comes to those who are ordinarily cheerful, a battle line is not the place to get annoyed. Their cheer will be taken away by the clamor of battle and gunfire. Since they haven't constantly groomed bravery in their guts, their usual willfulness doesn't come out, so they appear ordinary.

A dragon is a creature with the ultimate positive energy, so much so that it can fly in the sky without wings. Yet it usually remains curled up in supremely still waters. This is how a man with a heart of true martial courage constantly cultivates himself.

————

In latter days, in years of plenty when there is enough food, knights are badly off, while in bad years when food is insufficient, commoners starve. As those above and below suffer in turn, there is a trend toward social disorder. Why is that?

There are many reasons, but there are three main sources. One is that when cities great and small are situated in locations convenient to river and sea routes, extravagance grows daily and cannot be suppressed. The merchants prosper while the knights become impoverished.

Second, the practice of exchanging grain for goods has gradually disappeared, and when money is the only medium of exchange the prices of goods gradually rise. Everywhere the gold and silver passes into the hands of merchants, while the great and the small both suffer lack.

Third is the proliferation of interests and objects with no necessary reason. Knights convert the rice they receive as salary to purchase things. When the price of rice is low and the cost of goods is high, there is not enough to meet needs. If they have a lot of interests and acquire a lot of objects on top of that, they become even poorer. When knights are in financial distress, they increase their exactions from the commoners, who therefore suffer lack in years of plenty and starve and freeze in bad years. When the knights and commoners are broke, the artisans and peddlers can't trade them anything for grain. Only the big merchants get richer.

This is because the economic power is in the hands of commoners. Rulers of countries, masters of the world, should never lend wealth and nobility to other people, even temporarily. When they lend wealth and nobility to others, they lose their authority and the state ceases to exist. When the world is in chaos, the merchant's wealth is his own enemy; just as it is the tiger's stripes that bring trouble from hunters, it is the merchant's wealth that makes him captive to brigands and may even cost him his life.

Even plants and trees, which have no feelings, lose their leaves and wither when their time comes. The flourishing and decline of things is their natural condition; so how could those who concentrate on their own profit to the detriment of others last forever?

SIX

YAMAGA SOKO (1622–1685)

Yamaga Soko was a distant descendant of the noble Fujiwara clan, which had traditionally provided empresses and ministers of state for the imperial establishment. He himself, however, was born in far more humble circumstances, son of a samurai, born to a concubine. His father's patron was well connected, however, and after being relocated to the capital city of Edo, Yamaga was afforded the best educational opportunities available in his time.

A brilliant student even as a child, Yamaga had read the main texts of the official Confucian curriculum by the time he was eight years old. In his ninth year he was admitted to the school of Hayashi Razan, a neo-Confucian scholar patronized by the shogun. Recognized for his intelligence early on, Yamaga was already being solicited for service in the retinue of a feudal lord in his eleventh year. His father, however, would not permit this.

Yamaga began lecturing by invitation while still in his teens. In his fifteenth year he began to study military science and martial arts. He earned a professional license in this field by the age of twenty and began to teach five years later. During his late teens he also took up the study of Shinto, receiving instruction in several Shinto lineages. In the meantime, he was also lecturing on Confucian classics.

Remaining independent in spite of offers of employment, over the years Yamaga continued to broaden his studies, encompassing Zen and Taoism as well as the latest developments in neo-Confucianism, all the while lecturing and writing on military and political science.

Eventually Yamaga came to repudiate the neo-Confucian school of

Hayashi Razan officially upheld by the military government and was sent into exile for writing about his doubts. He also questioned classical Confucian ideology, considering it too idealistic, and ultimately evolved into a pragmatist. While acknowledging some value to all the ancient teachings he studied, Yamaga refused to consider any ideology as absolute and regarded classics useful to the extent that their underlying principles could be effectively adapted to contemporary conditions. His work was censored by the Shogunate and remained in manuscript with his descendants and disciples until he was rediscovered in modern times and came to be regarded as an icon of bushido.

■ ■ ■

Self-Admonitions

Rising early and retiring at midnight, being attentive to my father and mother, instructing my children and students, getting along with my relatives, taking care of my servants and dependents, meeting my guests, respecting men of will, pitying incompetents, studying literature when I have any energy left over from these activities—each of these is an aspiration of mine, but more in name than reality. Therefore I do not attain the limit of what is possible in anything I do. It is on this that I must make the most effort to examine myself.

I've never been able to exert myself to the utmost in looking after my parents. It's not that I just say it and don't think it, but in reality I'm not that attentive. It's easy to miss my regular duties to see that they're settled at night and to look in on them in the morning. Since my parents are old, there's not much time left to look after them—shouldn't I examine myself?

I give my children and students slight instruction and yet expect them to achieve. Without being earnest myself, I press them to be grave; without being correct myself, I want them to be correct. The reason my children and students don't improve is that I scarcely criticize myself.

The way I direct my servants and subordinates, I want them to work hard without rest. I expect everything of everyone, and I treat them as if I'm a lord. This is all because I take it easy, I just benefit myself, and I don't become knowledgeable. Inwardly I have no virtue or intelligence to influence them; outwardly I have no means of punishing or rewarding them. Why should they be loyal? If I force them to be loyal, they'll resent it to the end. Moreover, I am greedy, so when servants and subordinates speak of something that will profit me and enrich my house, I'm privately pleased. This is very shameful.

I treat my friends mostly as if they were not equal to me. Proud of my knowledge, I look down on them. Therefore in half a day of interaction I'm too familiar, not regulating it with manners. I'm not dignified or serious with them, ultimately becoming casual and flippant.

My judgments are biased by personal preferences, without caution. This demands particular self-examination. I agree too easily, because I'm proud of my knowledge and want others to praise me. Therefore things often go wrong because I don't make sure to understand them fully.

I've never admired utensils or objects, so, except for military equipment, I'm quite ignorant of their designs. Generally speaking, hobbies deprive you of will. To be too ignorant, though, is inadequacy. Utensils and objects are also necessary implements for people.

I am extremely simple by nature, poor in mannerly appearances, too frugal in dress, residence, and consumption. This is living simply and acting simple; should I study mannerly appearances thoroughly, think of how to attain proper measure, and make plans in that direction?

I'm influenced by gain and loss, so what I say can get clever, and I value speed and dispatch in what I do. Intent on establishing myself, I don't think of establishing others. With so little virtue, I wish to attain my ambitions. This is injurious to others, a disgraceful legacy. I am a criminal to heaven and earth! If the mandate of heaven doesn't favor me, isn't that appropriate? Why don't I think?

I am getting older and feebler daily, lazy about a lot of things, time and again neglecting work on military education and army formation. What is more, I'm getting more interested in political education day by day. It's an ancient warning that we forget danger when at ease—why don't I set my will on this?

To violate universal norms in order to make oneself pure is a false premise. To wish to establish oneself yet ignore the people is inhumane. To violate a former office to boost your own reputation is disloyalty. Not siding with your relatives because you want to make your own filial piety foremost is disrespectful. To be proud of having done a good deed is ignorance. To see what is right yet fail to do it is lack of courage.

Everything you say or do, every word you write, every implement you manage, manifests the totality that is there. Should we be self-aware?

I'm always forgetting myself—I really have to watch out for this. A lowly man from a poor family, I wish to be the same as distinguished guests from noble clans; wishing to prolong my life, I forget about death; evoking desires, I profit myself, forgetting the harm I'm doing to my body; advanced in years, I forget my vigor's declining; wishing to attain my aspirations, I forget that my knowledge is little and my virtue is slight.

I feel shame only for what outsiders see and hear, while being incautious about what my family, servants, and dependents know. Ashamed of what my family, servants, and dependents know, I don't consider what the supreme deity perceives. Generally, external affairs should be done through the agency of people who are familiar with the matters concerned, while internal matters should be viewed through the eyes of family, servants, and dependents. The appropriate ability and character should be developed by way of the teachings of sages. As for psychological impulses and the circumspection when sitting alone at home, these should be seen from the perspective of heaven and earth.

Time has momentum that cannot be forced. Confucius said, "Those who are ignorant but like to do things their own way, those who are mean but like to have things their own way, and those who while born in the present age revert to antiquated ways—these are people misfortune besets."

Zisi said, "Even with manners and means, without opportunity a noble man does not act."

Mencius said, "Even if you're intelligent, it's better to ride momentum. Even if you have a plow, it's best to wait for the season."

Admonitions to Children and Students

A person's support is found in clothing, food, housing, and everyday necessities.

Clothing is for protection against cold and heat and for the arrangement of mannerly appearances. Designed according to the type of work one does, the crude and the fine, the dyed and the embroidered, each has uses. And if you don't wear them correctly, your mind will also be unbalanced thereby. When you wear casual clothing your mind will be correspondingly slack, while if you wear formal clothing your mind will be controlled and alert. Therefore if you choose quality, design, and pattern according to the standard proprieties of dress, it will naturally help nourish your mood.

As for food and drink, they regulate satiety and hunger and nourish the physical body; each has proprieties of richness or plainness. Men of will are not ashamed of poor food. When you eat your fill and dress warmly, you invariably get lazy at work. If you are slovenly and inconsiderate while eating and drinking, you lose a courteous appearance. If you do not eat and drink at regular times but follow your whims, then you'll lose the balance of fullness and hunger.

Housing keeps out moisture, wind, rain, and dew, enables people to gather together, lets people rest, and provides a place for things. While kept austere, it should be socially suitable. It is an ancient admonition that the abode affects the mood. Water is basically the same, but depending on the location it may be muddy, flowing or still, far-reaching or short-ranged, naturally differing in each situation. How can we be careless about where we live? Whatever things we use in our daily activities, our mental energy lodges there, like a movable object. If you examine principles to perfect manners and arrange forms for full functionality, then they can nurture your spirits.

For you children and students to discipline yourselves is all a matter of being careful about what you look at and listen to. Looking and listening are where the mind first moves. Therefore you should maintain a proper manner and facial expression and not look or listen casually. When your eyes are rolling, you're not looking straight; and when you lean over to listen, your listening is unmannerly. Therefore your mind is stirred by this.

As for speech, the rule is to be minimal, while circumspection is prudence; say what you have to say, reply what you must reply, keeping deference in mind and acknowledging the company before you speak. If your facial expression is not genuine as well, people will get the impression of falsehood.

In general, to be quick to speak, prefer clever talk, and make a thing of eloquence is the flaw of self-assertive flippancy. Always beware of talk that is vulgar, weak, indulgent, calculating, commercial, lascivious, or hedonistic, and don't talk or joke about the mistakes of government or the evils of other people. In your written correspondence, you don't need classic quotations and shouldn't use unconventional prose or unusual characters. Give thorough consideration to what is appropriate for the time, with careful attention to formal courtesies—don't be too ready to change customary courtesies based on your own literary talent. This is what is meant by the saying that manners and music are not matters of personal debate.

Always examine yourselves, recognize where your temperament is unstable and where it is stable, and what your strengths and weaknesses are; reduce excesses and foster what is insufficient. In matters of leisure, let others go first; in matters of labor, be first yourself. What warriorhood requires as duty, moreover, is in this one thing above all—in emergencies and combat you shouldn't defer to others.

The Way lies in each aspect of your everyday conduct and activity. For knights to think only of military maneuvers to the neglect of ordinary manners is not the bravery of a noble man.

If you sit rigidly for a long time, your legs will become numb and it will be hard to get up and run in an emergency. If you keep your hands in your pockets fearing they'll freeze in the cold, or if you apply antichapping ointment, in either case they'll be hard to use in a hurry. If the movements of your hands and feet are not lively, you'll be useless as warriors. But if the movements of your hands and feet are unrestrained, then you'll lack decorum. This is all a matter of training your hands and feet and making your body accustomed to being mannerly.

The body is where the mind resides. Considering mannerly appearances in movement, standing still, sitting, and reclining, in your facial expression, tone of voice, where you face, and where you step, if you don't act at random your mind will then be orderly. "Don't look at anything improper, don't listen to anything improper, don't say anything improper, don't do anything improper."

[SEVEN]

KAIBARA EKKEN (1630–1714)

Kaibara Ekken was a son of a physician in the service of a feudal lord. He began to read at the age of nine. At first he was attracted to Buddhism, but by the time he was fourteen he was dissuaded from this path by his elder brother, who was his tutor in Confucian studies. Returning to Confucianism, Ekken aspired to become a physician and spent a number of years studying medicine in Kyoto, the imperial capital. In 1661 he returned to his native place to practice medicine, but then he became a professional Confucian scholar. In this latter capacity he served three successive lords over a period of forty years. He traveled all over Japan, and in 1700 retired from public service to live in Kyoto, where he died at an advanced age.

Kaibara is careful to distinguish the warrior creed of self-sacrifice from a crude cult of death and to dissociate the way of warfare from a doctrine of winning by whatever means. He was particularly concerned with what he saw as a tendency to carry the latter ideology over into ordinary life, using any means available, regardless of social or moral probity, to gain an advantage.

In this connection he emphasized the importance of education and ethics, while nevertheless maintaining a lively interest in military tactics. Effective organization and strategy, he believed, are sounder routes to victory than the energy of unbridled opportunism, in that they enable leaders to maintain sobriety in the process of conflict while providing for better reintegration of society in the aftermath of warfare than would unethical methods of attack.

69

In terms of his sense of civil society and moral structure, Kaibara is normally Confucian in outlook. In his conceptual and practical lessons on military tactics, Kaibara emphasizes Taoist aspects of traditional Chinese military science. Here his writings evince traces of a vociferous debate with contemporaries who favored what they described as the more aggressive Japanese manner of warfare in comparison with the cautious and reserved approach of the Chinese classics that Kaibara preferred.

■ ■ ■

It is not hard for knights to sacrifice themselves in combat. As for the bravery of bloodlust, even bandits can exercise this. What is hard is to sacrifice oneself for justice. Therefore to die when you shouldn't is to disregard your body, and to mistreat the body received from your parents is impious. If you don't die when you should, on the other hand, this is fearing death and clinging to life, failing to serve your lord, so it is disloyalty.

———

Military methods differ in scale of function according to rank, depending on whether one is a commander or a knight. One should first learn what is critical to one's rank. Commanders, of course, and heads of offices and soldiers as well, cannot deal with organization unless they know military methods. Grandees and men of higher ranks have to know military methods.

Military methods are the root of martial arts. If you only study archery, riding, swordsmanship, and spear fighting without learning military methods, this is not military science. This is like enjoying the arts without knowing the basis, losing your will as you amuse yourself with things. Martial arts are techniques of individual combat; military methods are techniques of opposing masses of men.

———

People who study Japanese military methods without cultural learning are ignorant of principle. They teach people that the

Japanese warrior's way should not apply the principles of humaneness, justice, loyalty, and faith like Confucians, that victory cannot be won without falsehood and deception. They also say that warfare is all about success, that people like Cao Cao in China and Ashikaga Takauji of Japan ignored humanity and justice and usurped others' countries, but this is the real motive of a military leader. As for the likes of Zhuge Kongming of China and Kusunoki Masashige of Japan, though they were loyal and just they failed to succeed, and this is not what military command is about. War is a path of deception, depending on the trend of events at a given time; one may even exercise strategic deception on one's own allies, usurping the achievements of others. Or else, there is no harm in throwing a country into disorder to take it over by subversion. This is the Japanese warrior way. The Japanese warrior way can hardly be practiced the Chinese way. As Japan is a martial country, it is impossible to succeed by China's straightforward, sluggish manner, as it does not suit Japanese customs. Wily and sharp, taking the credit for others' achievements, stealing the heads cut off by others to claim one's own bravery—this is the Japanese warrior way, so they say, teaching this to people secretly.

When people who hear this are uneducated and unwise, they don't know how it's wrong. They believe it and think it's true, so even in normal times they employ the strategies of military tactics, using deception to make gains. There are a lot of people with this attitude. Most people who study warfare are deluded by this.

———

When among people, if anyone is impolite or insulting to you, as long as it is not a dishonor you should put up with it, pretending you didn't hear it. You wouldn't really want to get into an angry argument with that ignoramus.

However, if he doesn't understand this and arrogantly looks down on you thinking he has shamed you, then, considering the concern that he might embarrass you again another day, call him out where no one's around and rebuke him.

If you are insulted in the presence of others, you shouldn't get angry even if it happens twice. You should respond with the truth. If the person doesn't accept the truth, then rebuke him sternly. Don't insult him back.

People who inconsiderately insult others in contempt are fools; they don't think about disastrous consequences. They are invariably timid, insubstantial imbeciles, so if you rebuke them firmly they'll shut up.

Even so, you shouldn't contemptuously insult people yourself, because no matter how timid they may be, if they get angry they may go ahead and fight. If you fight with someone who's lost control of himself, even if you win you'll have to commit suicide.

———

Good commanders in ancient times did not excel only in bravery, ferocity, strategy, and tactics. They used both culture and arms, exercised both leniency and ferocity. Humane and loving, they pardoned minor errors, forgot old injuries, listened carefully to criticism and put it to use. They were generous in rewarding merit, without boasting of themselves. Therefore the officers and soldiers united in harmony, enabling them to achieve success.

———

The *Annals of Mr. Lu* says, "Rulers of moribund countries are invariably arrogant, assured of their own wisdom, and contemptuous of people." Such was the death of Oda Nobunaga.

Lord Nobunaga was outstanding in history for martial bravery, but most of the opponents he destroyed in achieving his success were not unjust. Regrettably, it's simply that he became arrogant and contemptuous of knights, so Akechi [Mitsuhide 1526–1582] became resentful and angry. Because Oda thought he had his own wisdom, he relied on his own intelligence alone and refused criticism and advice; so Hirate [Masahide, 1492–1553], his secretary of state, unable to advise him or remonstrate with him, committed suicide. Because Oda thought little of people, he was contemptuous of opponents and unafraid. When he incautiously camped with a small contingent in a place without natural barriers, Akechi found out he was unprepared and made a surprise attack. Oda couldn't fend him off and got killed.

Sayings of ancients that are logical never miss the mark.

———

In a contest with an opponent, premature boldness is not valued; calmly holding back is valued. This is the way to overcome enemies.

But it is hard to hold back. Holding back means patience. Facing an opponent, hold back calmly; don't make the first move in haste. If you are too bold to hold back and so hasty that you make the first move, your opponent will see your slipup and strike, so you'll get beat.

When two men fight, before it is clear who's going to win and who's going to lose, if you watch your opponent's movements and strike the gaps, it's easy to win. For this reason the first to make a move loses, while the one who follows up wins.

Holding back is indeed an art of war whose one word is worth a thousand pieces of gold. It should not be disregarded. This is a doctrine of the ancients. As it says in *Three Strategies*, "Change and movement are inconstant, evolving according to the opponent, not taking the initiative but adapting to what happens." If you're too quick and make the first move, you're likely to get beat.

It's hard to hold back and not move. That is why the ability to hold back is important. You shouldn't act impulsively. If you make moves at random without perceiving an advantage, you're likely to lose. A noble man controls frivolity with gravity, awaits action in a state of calm. It is important for the spirit to be whole, the mood steady, and the mind unmoving.

———

A man of courage is not outwardly rough. He should be, as Xunzi says, "able to be calm, then able to respond." That means that when facing an opponent you can win by calming your mind and not letting it stir. If you get excited at the drop of a hat, you have no internal basis for responding to opponents, so you won't be able to overcome people.

———

Brave and fierce men of old who were excellent commanders may have been successful in war and founded states, but without wisdom it is impossible to preserve culture, keep secure, and hand on the legacy to posterity. Therefore a warrior leader considers wisdom first; courage is next to that.

———

A man of old said, "Victory in war is a matter of cohesion, not numbers." This means that winning in warfare is a matter of officers and soldiers obeying the commander, so orders are not disregarded, all join forces together as one, and they fight selflessly.

An army is not to be relied upon just because it is big. If the officers and soldiers do not take to the commander but disobey and desert, since they don't work together and unite as one, even with a million men an army can't win.

———

In the use of arms, martial dignity is certainly important. Without humaneness and justice, however, the hearts of the men won't go along. Then it is impossible to mobilize warriors.

———

The battles of a good general are well planned and carefully thought out; they win when it is easy to win. Therefore not a lot of officers and soldiers get killed. Ignorant generals and benighted leaders, not knowing this principle, delight in large numbers of deaths on both sides. This is not only inhumane, it is due to stupidity in military procedure.

Superior warriors consider it best to win without fighting. If a fight is unavoidable, a good commander is skilled in the ways of war and has strategy, so he doesn't get a lot of people killed, whether enemies or allies.

A man of old said, "After three generations of generals, a family will have no posterity." The meaning of this is that the Way of Heaven hates inhumanity and does not like killing. Since everyone under heaven is a child of heaven, as it hates the killing of its children, if you like to kill people your own posterity dies out.

Even if they become generals, humane men do not kill a lot of people. If so, what would be the harm in generations of generals? As for men who are inhumane and have killed a lot of people, it doesn't necessarily take three generations—there are a lot of examples past and present of men who became generals and whose posterity ended in one generation. This is how it can be known that the Way of Heaven detests inhumanity.

When battling opponents, if you are excessive in beating them, they'll lash back and fight powerfully. So stop at the first victory. This may seem lax, but there will be no disaster in the aftermath.

Even in an argument between ordinary men, if one vilifies the other too much and is excessive in beating him down, he'll wind up the loser if the other man can't put up with it and retaliates vehemently.

The art of war of good commanders of ancient times involved no massive victory and no massive defeat. This is a good commander's art of war. Commanders who don't know the art of war may score tremendous victories by luck, but they also incur many huge losses. This is the not the way a good commander employs a military force.

Point men should also act with this understanding. If you manage to penetrate deeply by yourself, you may be lucky enough to achieve something, but many are helplessly killed by the enemy.

When an argument turns into a fight, it always comes from contention. Contention means rebuking another's excessive words and discourtesy, refusing to tolerate them. If you tolerate them, there is no contention, no enemy, and no disgrace. When dealing with people, it is imperative to be polite in speech and manner, avoiding discourtesy.

The way for a commander to deploy an army in combat should include four things: justice, technique, courage, and knowledge.

First, justice should be considered the substance. When you start a war, you have to examine whether it is just or unjust. If your military order is organized and your army is strong, you are sure to beat your opponent, but if the adversary is not one that ought to be attacked, then it is unjust to start a war. War should not be instigated. This means making justice the substance.

Next, technique is essential to prosecute warfare. Technique refers to the principles of preparing battle formations and means of overcoming opponents. If you don't know the techniques of warfare, you cannot prevail over opponents. Everything should be done with due attention to technique, but this is particularly true of warfare, since it is a matter of life and death, survival or destruction—you have to know how. If you battle without technique, you'll invariably lose.

Next, courage is essential to prosecute warfare. Without courage, there is no power, no force, to defeat enemies.

It must also be done with knowledge. Without knowledge, a military action is unsuccessful from start to finish. Therefore the path of warfare begins with knowledge and ends with knowledge.

Whenever a noble man uses arms, these four elements must all be included.

Among five kinds of warfare, war for justice and war for defense are used by noble men. War out of anger, war out of pride, and war out of greed are not used by noble men; they are used by small men.

Military action ought to be undertaken on the basis of humanity and justice. This means employing cultured warriors. If you make war unsupported by cultured warriors, you can't avoid making men into bandits.

Ordinarily, making war is contrary to the benevolent heart of the universe that gives birth to beings. Sages use arms only when unavoidable. This is implementation of the principle of nature. The warfare of sages is an exercise in justice; humaneness is therein. The sense of man using weaponry is expressed in Master Cheng's verse on termites: "To kill them offends humaneness; to let them proliferate is an injury to justice."

[EIGHT]

NAGANUMA MUNEYOSHI (1635–1690)

Naganuma Muneyoshi was a neo-Confucian and a military scientist of the Koshu or Takeda school. Many lords requested him to teach, but he acceded to only a few such requests, and then would always lecture on Confucian classics before touching on military science.

Very much the classicist in matters of military science, Naganuma reflects a typically Taoist attitude toward arms, acknowledging necessity but abjuring aggression. He defines seven kinds of just warfare, while condemning predatory warfare in pursuit of reputation or profit. In this connection he criticizes a popular tendency to admire the power of violence without question of ethical probity or purpose.

■ ■ ■

The Origins of the Military

In ancient times states had civil and military offices, and ministers and generals had separate jobs.

The ministers assisted the ruler above, ordering yin and yang according to the four seasons to bring about what was best for all people. Internally they oversaw the hundred bureaus, making the nobles, grandees, and scholars responsible for their respective duties and comforting the peasants, enabling widows, widowers, orphans, and childless each to find their place. Externally they won the allegiance of allies, so that the feudal lords maintained order and didn't start any wars. They reassured other peoples on all sides, so the other peoples agreed to diplomacy, and those beyond the seas admired the civilization. Therefore ministers are the guts and heart of a nation.

As for generals, they receive their orders at the national shrine, entrusted with a share of authority in the field, in sole charge of the threat of arms, leading the hearts of the armies, uniting the strength of the warriors. Thereby they overcome the unruly and punish the unjust. When their rage takes form, order prevails over a thousand miles; when their threat is exercised, all people submit. Therefore the generals are the claws and fangs of a nation.

This is like the production and destruction of yin and yang, by which the four seasons proceed. Yang is benevolence, yin is threat; when threat and benevolence are both effective, the people submit. If there is benevolence without threat, the people will be contemptuous and unruly. If there is threat without benevolence, the people will abscond in resentment. So neither one of these can be neglected.

Punitive attack and benevolent defense were the means by which the Yellow Emperor became ruler. Cultivating benevolence while neglecting arms was how the Chengsang tribe lost its territory. Those who are violent, oppressive, and brutal cannot win the hearts of the masses; that is why Xiang of Chu, after repeated attempts at oppressive acquisition, finally suffered disgrace at Raven River. Those who maintain rituals but don't know about military power abandon their people that way; this is why Xiang of Song, by failing to attack an unprepared enemy, got defeated at the Hong River.

Enlightened rulers and wise generals will take lessons from these examples, internally cultivating cultural virtues while externally managing military preparations. When inside and outside are both provided for and the normal and the provisional are employed at appropriate times, then the nation can be preserved forever so the people will always be at peace.

Critique of Arms

"Weapons are instruments of ill omen." War is a dangerous affair. When used to settle the troubles of the world and eliminate harm to the people, warfare is just. Attacking innocent cities and killing innocent people is predatory warfare.

Predators are eager to mobilize, whereas noble men do so only when unavoidable. How could humane people be glad when armies are mobilized for aggressive attack while the people do not enjoy the benefits of benevolent government? It is the worst disaster.

Therefore when the founder of the Shang dynasty deposed the corrupt ruler of the Xia dynasty, even though the people of Xia were relieved, it was an embarrassment to virtue. When the founder of the Zhou dynasty attacked the degenerate ruler of the Shang dynasty, though the soldiers on the front lines switched their allegiance to him, this was still not perfectly good. This is because he did not humbly accept abdication but acquired the empire by conquest.

Though operations of sages respond to nature, accord with humanity, and execute justice throughout the land, rescuing the people from trouble, still sages are ashamed of not being as virtuous as the ancients. They also fear that coming generations will use them as an excuse to become anarchistic.

In later ages, rulers and commanders largely employed arms to usurp territory and profit economically. This is unnatural and inhumane, but they had no shame. Killing countless innocents, ending countless lives, they cared for nothing but to expand their territory and increase their power. How are they different from bandits in this? Their conduct of affairs was entirely dependent on what power could accomplish, without considering where justice lay.

Therefore, before they attained power they had overtly behaved benevolently and stood for justice to win the allegiance of the gentry and the masses. Once they got power, they assassinated their lords, banished their fathers, killed their sons, and duped their relatives, all in pursuit of their desires.

These are called rebellious ministers and usurping sons. Even if there are emperors or overlords above them, they do not punish them for assassination, for fear of their power. So they become accustomed to acting with impunity and consider destruction and depredation normal. Taking over the small and swallowing the weak, ultimately they get to the point of usurping the whole land.

When later people don't criticize these crimes but go along with them and praise them, this is of the gravest concern to good generals and wise rulers. This is using instruments of ill omen for violence and disruption, starting a dangerous business that destroys both soldiers and civilians. The cruelty and viciousness in that is impossible to express in words. When the corruption of latter-day militarists verges on this, we should not fail to take a warning.

Just War

The origins of warfare are of many types, but they do not go beyond three categories: just war, contest for prestige, or greed for profit.

When it is humane, just, loyal, and faithful, harboring no selfishness, an operation that is in accord with nature and humanity is called a just war.

There are seven kinds of just war in all. First is when the people all over the land are withering away under a brutal government, waiting for the time when it will some day perish, so Providence accedes to the people's desire and borrows the services of a spiritual warrior with the character of a sage to execute the tyrant, so the people are revived in the midst of water and fire.

Second is when there is a virtuous ruler with no resentful citizens in his domain, but rebels infringe upon the king's authority, antagonizing his allies, not responding to invitations to make peace and not submitting to admonitions about justice. When it is unavoidable, the ruler commands the overlords and orders allies to raise an army to wipe out the rebels.

Third is when treacherous ministers assassinate their rulers, and loyal ministers and dutiful knights raise an army for justice to execute them.

Fourth is when the ruler is weak while the ministers are strong; authority rests with the powerful, who confer private favors to establish a commanding presence; troublesome people form factions; and the country is on the brink of collapse. Then loyal ministers contrive to stabilize the nation.

Fifth is when the whole land is already in chaos, disloyal strongmen carve out their own bailiwicks and invade each other, and then the loyal and the good assist the ruling house to restore the central government and rescue the people's lives.

Sixth is when there are those who seek revenge on the enemies of their fathers and grandfathers, who take pains to humble themselves to servants, attract heroes, and enlist death-defying warriors, raising an army to efface a national disgrace.

Seventh is when the country is in utter chaos and has no settled ruler, so everyone keeps to his stronghold, waiting for the world to settle down; if bandits come spoiling, robbing your people, then you raise an army to hunt them down, to relieve the people of their harm.

When an enemy afflicts you and you have no choice but to take action, this is called responsive war. This means victory by military response. When it saves the world from disaster and gets rid of what harms the populace, then it is considered just warfare. Those whose warfare is just prosper because they pursue the people's happiness.

When a pretense of justice is used to seek a reputation, this is warfare in a contest for prestige. An armed contest is dangerous; to pursue prestige thereby is to forget justice.

When a pretense of humanity and justice is used for profiteering, that is treacherous warfare. Those who arm out of greed will perish, because this is unnatural and inhuman. In latter days this type of treachery is not rare. There are those who outwardly claim to have a just cause in executing usurping assassins, while inwardly harboring a scheme to set themselves up, eventually getting rid of the heirs of the ruler and killing the loyal ministers.

These are bandits robbing bandits—how can they escape blame? Some overtly say they want to effect good government throughout the land, leaving a reputation for merit in the books, but in reality they wind up assassinating their fathers and murdering their sons, then increasing taxes and exactions so much that they lose the masses. This is severing the root in pursuit of the branches. How could they not collapse and perish?

People of the world do not discuss whether they are just or unjust but simply praise the cunning who take by aggression and have won battles repeatedly, calling them heroes and good commanders. Noble men despise prestige that is wrongly acquired.

Planning for the Nation

The root of the land is in the nation, the root of the nation is in the home, the root of the home is in the person. Therefore those who would peacefully govern the land, the nation, and the home first cultivate themselves. When you are personally cultivated, then your whole household is influenced by this; if this is extended, the whole nation is orderly. If one nation is orderly, the whole land will go along with it. This is how a ruler, by personal conduct, leads subordinates by means of his character, so the people, observing, are impressed and their hearts submit.

Because he treats the people humanely, the people cleave to their ruler, considering his benevolence. Because he balances them with courtesies, the upper and lower classes are defined and not confused. Because he inspires them with duty, the people have a sense of shame and are completely loyal, even at the cost of their lives. Because he awes them with law, the people are afraid to infringe. Because he motivates them with faith, he evokes sincerity by being sincere, and the people do not deviate from their constancy.

In this way a nation grows rich and strong, the people secure and happy. If something happens, they are able to fight and are firm in defense. Therefore rival states submit to this awesome virtue, and the whole land accepts its authority.

Three Essentials

In general, the way to govern a nation is to nurture the life of the people, restore the nature of the people, and prevent the people from doing wrong. These are the three essentials.

Equalize land allotments, minimize taxes, employ the people at the appropriate times, have the people plant mulberry and flax. When the farmers till, the women spin silk, the people don't waste their time, and the state doesn't waste land, then there is enough clothing and food so that there's no anxiety about supporting parents, wives, and children. The people are constant, and robbery and banditry don't occur in the territory. The state is tranquil, the people are at peace. Because of this, merchants gather and make markets, artisans come and make utensils; the needs of the nation are fully met, so the people are prosperous and happy. This is called nurturing the life of the people.

If you nurture them without educating them, the people won't know about courtesy and duty. Without courtesy, social order will be disturbed; without duty, the ruler is disregarded.

The way to educate the people is to set up schools in districts and villages, establish colleges in prefectures and provinces, provide officials in charge of instruction, equip them with books, set aside a budget for expenses, admit the children and youth of the gentry and populace, and teach them. In the schools have them study writing and arithmetic and read classics and literature. In the colleges have them analyze ideograms and discuss their meanings. Enable everyone to know how to investigate things to acquire knowledge, cultivate oneself, and govern others. Thus does a nation develop customs of respect for parents, fraternity, loyalty, faith, courtesy, duty, and integrity. This is called restoring the nature of the people.

Even with education and sustenance, there is law; if the people's wrongs are not prevented, then dishonesty will develop and the nation will become disorderly. Therefore the provinces, prefectures, districts, and villages should all have offices to which intelligent and conscientious people are promoted, appointing them according to their character to determine legal prohibitions and make their stipulations known, to assist in government and education, so people won't get into trouble. If any violate the law, then indictments are composed, complete with the reasons, and they are exposed to the public in the marketplace, to keep the masses of people in line. This is called preventing the people from doing wrong.

When clothing and food are sufficient, the people are happy and don't think of rebelling. When the state provides education, the people know their duties and don't act against their leaders. When wrongdoing is prevented, crooks and schemers don't arise. If your government is like this, you have no rivals on earth.

Essentials of Warfare

In a discourse on warfare, Master Xun wrote, "What is essential is the allegiance of the people." In the military force of a humane man, superiors and subordinates are of one mind, the three armies combine their strength. The ministers are to their ruler, and the subordinates to their superiors, like sons and younger brothers working for their fathers and elder brothers, like the hands and arms shielding the head and eyes and protecting the chest and abdomen. So for warfare the allegiance of the people is essential.

The way wise leaders and intelligent commanders govern subordinates is to inspire sincerity by being sincere. Thus the feelings of superiors and subordinates are united. Appreciation of benevolence and submission to duty lead to the will to sacrifice one's life for the country out of gratitude. It is after this that squads can be organized, orders can be issued, instructions for siege and combat can be given, rewards and penalties can be put into effect.

Generally, when advance and retreat and response and engagement follow the will of the commander and there is no deviation from the system of signals, this means superiors and subordinates are of one mind, the strength of the three armies is united.

If officers and soldiers have no personal allegiance, then even if you try to train them they won't practice, and when you issue orders, they won't obey; if you punish them, they're resentful, while if you reward them they get greedy. The military loses its aim, in battle it violates morality. How can you gain victory that way?

This happens when you are affectionate toward the people without really being sincere, and so the soldiers feel no personal allegiance to you.

It says in some text, "It is like taking care of a baby. If you can truly love the people with the feeling of one caring for an infant, then who would not cleave to you?" When those above love those below, then those below feel kinship with those above. Therefore those above and below are one in mind. When their minds are one, their energies are coordinated; when their energies are coordinated, their strength is united. When their strength is united, ten can attack a hundred, a thousand can attack ten thousand. If the members of all three military forces combine their strength, who in the world would dare stand up to them?

So it is said, when the ruler of a nation likes humaneness, it has no enemies in the world. People take to the quality of humaneness like water flows downward; they come to be subjects without being summoned, they submit diplomatically without being attacked.

Disciplined Order

Master Qi said, "Without disciplined order, military operations are impossible." It seems to me that an army without disciplined order is very weak in force of arms and so is easily defeated in encounters with enemies. A disciplined army can beat an undisciplined army even three to five times its size.

Suppose there is a huge boulder that dozens of men cannot roll. Now, if one man gives a call so that the group responds in unison, pushing at once, even a few men can move it. There is no technique to this but coordinating efforts as one.

Order in an army is also like this. That is because disciplined order is a means of coordinating energetic force and momentum. The essence is in harmony—so when you have the personal allegiance of the knights and commoners, then you can speak of disciplined order; when disciplined order is established, then you can speak of combat.

In practice, ordered discipline begins with selecting officers and is stabilized by the formation of teams, regulated by prohibitions and commands, controlled by pennants, moved and stopped by cymbals and drums, divided and joined by banners, transformed by surprise and convention. Then victories are complete.

Generally speaking, when armed forces attain complete victory in battle, it comes from being fully equipped with method and technique. Without method and technique, even if a commander is intelligent and courageous he cannot sustain superiority.

This is like the example of Li Guang, who "could win the allegiance of warriors by being lenient and not cruel, was unmatched in talent and energy, and so could fight," and yet Wei Qing considered him hapless and wouldn't put him in charge of the forward army because his troops had no order and were repeatedly surrounded by the Huns.

Cheng Bushi said, "Guang's army is extremely simple, so when the Hunnish soldiers break through its ranks, it has no way to stop them. His officers and soldiers are also easygoing, though all of them are willing to die for him. As for my army, even when it's thrown into disarray the Huns still can't break through our ranks."

He Mengchun said, "If you emulate Cheng Bushi, even if unsuccessful you still won't be beaten. Those who emulate Li

Guang rarely escape defeat and destruction." If an army dispenses with disciplined order, even the distinguished talent of a Li Guang cannot be considered a model, to say nothing of lesser men.

In our country, Minamoto Yoshitsune was a commander who won a hundred percent of his battles; he appeared unexpectedly, took advantage of confusion, and never let an enemy's vulnerability slip by. His movements were secretive and sudden as a spirit. Nevertheless, the victories he managed to achieve were solely dependent on his own bravery and talent, as he had no system of order. He can't be taken as a model either.

What Sun Tzu calls skill at warfare is taking a stand on invincible ground while not missing the enemy's vulnerabilities. Disciplined order is up to oneself, that is all. If you gain victory without discipline, this should be called being lucky you didn't lose.

The technique of disciplined order involves principles for selecting officers, to distribute tasks according to abilities. Therefore when the right people are put in charge, a battle formation is already set. The principles of teaming are defined, so there is no worry about confusion and conflict in the ranks. Therefore regulating a multitude is like regulating a small group. With a system of pennants and drums to alert the eyes and ears of the three armies and control their movements, it is possible to direct a multitude like directing a small group. When prohibitions and orders are promulgated uniting the minds of the three armies, the brave cannot advance alone and the timid cannot retreat alone.

When the military is run like this, the energy of the armies is naturally unified. When energy is unified, strength is uniform. When strength is uniform, momentum is maximized, so that wherever it touches collapses and whatever it strikes crumbles. This is what is meant by a disciplined army winning every battle.

The Harm in Warfare

The benefit and harm in warfare have extremely important implications. That is why Master Sun says, "War is a grave matter for a nation, a ground of life or death, a way to survival or destruction, which must be examined." Generally speaking, if it is prosecuted only when unavoidable, it is just. Just warfare is beneficial to the populace, so the people of the nation are glad of it and the whole world supports it. Due to this the military is harmonious and the nation is strong, its prosperity transmitted to posterity. There is no greater benefit from warfare than this.

Making war because you want to do so is greed. Greedy war harms the populace, so the people of the country suffer from it and the whole world hates it. Due to this the military is disgraced and the nation is endangered, its disaster afflicting posterity. There is no greater harm in warfare than this.

This is natural, so the distinction between justice and profit must be examined.

The benefit and harm that wars do to nations are like the benefit and harm of water and fire for people. People cannot do without water and fire for a single day, but when misused they are more harmful than anyone can say. The benefit and harm in warfare are also like this. Therefore the *Spring and Autumn* tradition says, "Warfare is like fire; if you don't contain it, you'll burn yourself."

As for the use of arms, there may be a domestic uprising, or an attack from a neighboring country—then a militia is raised to put a stop to violent disorder, so as to relieve the people's distress. When the rebels have been subdued or the aggressors repelled, then the military forces are withdrawn but kept strictly prepared as a national guard. This is proper measure in use of arms.

Military action with proper measure helps the nation more than words can say. Military action without proper measure harms the nation, also more than words can say. So when you discuss the benefit of military action, first you should discuss the harm of military action. If you only look at the benefit without considering the harm, you'll slip into greedy warfare.

A military that is greedy attacks innocent cities and kills innocent people, usurps others' land to increase its own power. This is called a bandit army. A bandit army may overcome people for a while by force, but people will be alienated, ghosts and spirits will undermine it, and in the end no profit will be realized.

Tempering the Heart

The job of a knight is to honor civic virtues and take care of military duties, devoting himself with complete loyalty to the defense of the nation. That is because civic and military matters are like outside and inside; if either one is neglected, you cannot fulfill the path of knighthood.

A bird can fly because of the flapping of two wings; a chariot can travel because of the rolling of two wheels. The character of a knight has civic and military components. So it is said, "Arms are the sprouts of warriorhood, culture is the seed—if you don't get the seed, how can you cultivate the sprouts?"

Humaneness and courtesy are civic virtues; duty and courage are martial virtues. Knowing how to exercise virtues is intelligence; sincerity in their exercise is faith. These six qualities are not brought in from outside—they are intrinsic to our nature, inherent in the mind. When you use this mind, you survive; neglect this mind and you perish.

If a knight neglects arms, he's not worth talking about; if he neglects culture and doesn't cultivate it, he does not fully qualify as a knight.

Faith is critical to both culture and warfare. Without faith, humaneness is a mere expedient, courtesy degenerates into flattery, intelligence is decorated with deception, duty serves adventurism, and bravery deteriorates into violence and depredation. None of these are virtues.

If a knight has faith, then in times of peace he can assist the process of civilization, while in times of disturbance he can eliminate what injures the people. Then he is able to be a protector of the nation.

Knights keep their discipline to the death. Those whose aim is justice are best; those whose aim is honor are lesser. The custom of knights in Japan is to be extremely desirous of honor, so there are those who mistakenly think the desire for honor is itself justice. All in all, to carry out justice and thus achieve honor is good, while to perform exploits hoping to get honored is lowly. Even more so is aspiring only to get paid—even if you perform feats in battle, you are not worthy of being considered a knight.

To have a sense of shame is close to justness. A sense of shame means you criticize yourself. To seek fame is far from just. Seeking means the mind is outside, so you operate many strategies, create false pretenses, and concentrate on show, becoming less real in fact day by day. How can you have what you seek? This is what is called ruination by seeking to have everything.

Mr. Ma of Fufeng said, "When a subject serves in office for his lord, the surrounding glory is all the benevolence of the ruler; if one does not aspire to requite the nation, how can this be loyal?" It seems to me that when subjects serve their lord, if the intelligent use their minds to the full and the ignorant use their strength to the full, then their loyalty can be undivided. As for those who act for profit and fame, even if they single-handedly clear up problems for the country and benefit the state, since their motive is not duty, one can only speak of their accomplishment, one cannot praise their loyalty.

Loyalty is not just a matter of following orders forgetful of self, sacrifice for the country forgetful of home, crossing swords with enemies, and keeping your moral standards to the death in the face of difficulty. It is a matter of doing your duty without seeking to be honored for it, to be completely loyal without planning to profit from it, to safeguard your lord without worrying about demeaning yourself, to be unwilling to gloat even if you become successful and famous, to control yourself and be careful of your character, wishing to dedicate your life to the welfare of the nation, fulfilling the discipline of ministering to others.

Mencius said, "Who does no service? Serving your parents is the root of service. Who has no responsibility? Taking responsibility for yourself is the root of responsibility." If you serve your parents without respect, how can loyalty be transferred to your lord, how can obedience be transferred to your superiors? If you are not loyal and obedient to your lord and superiors, a wise ruler wouldn't accept you even if you have courage and talent. If you don't take genuine responsibility for yourself, how can you be responsible on the job and protect the country? Even if you put forth all your effort, a good general wouldn't employ you.

The way to be responsible for yourself is to seek peace of mind, that's all. You can't be happy accepting a salary when you don't do your duty, or being rewarded without having accomplished anything. You cannot be at ease with a reputation you have not earned or a position you do not deserve. If you see what's right but don't do it, you're disgraced by your cowardice; if you don't have the courage to die for your principles, then you'll be vexed by the shame of passivity and softness. If you perform your job without loyalty, you'll be criticized for not earning your pay. If you hide wrongs you've already done, you'll be in fear of exposure. So your mind won't be settled, and you'll always feel uneasy.

In addition, if you forget your duty because you get angry one day, or neglect your obligations for a momentary advantage, you will be pointed out and criticized by loyal ministers and dutiful knights. Even if you're thick-skinned, how could you endure that embarrassment?

You can never tell, moreover, when divine punishment might arrive. How can you have peace of mind? If one who is a knight always sacrifices his life and forgets gain for principle and justice, then as an individual he has nothing to be ashamed of at heart. Wouldn't this feel good?

Calculating and comparing gain and loss is a normal human feeling. If you know how to pursue gain and avoid loss yet do not observe whether it is right to do something or not, then you'll hastily rush to whatever is advantageous or convenient for yourself. People like this invariably ignore gratitude and disregard their ruler, turn their backs on duty and bring on invaders.

If you consider knowing where duty lies to be gain, and consider not doing your duty to be loss, this is close to being unaffected by danger and difficulty and not falling under the spell of profit.

Once you've erred in word or deed, don't pursue it. You should be careful of impulses in your mind beforehand. If you are not decisive before the fact, you won't be able to manage the impulse, so you should first control haste in everyday life.

In developing courage, combine justness and honesty, and you get balance and uprightness. If you foster bravery alone, the mood you build up will be too excessive, so the sense of fear will be gradually covered, and you'll become coarse and violent. This is harmful. A good general has no use for this.

If people can cultivate this courageous justness, then even if they haven't gone to war their hearts are brave, decisive, free of hesitancy. If you still can't help being hesitant, you haven't cultivated this adequately; you may not be able to be brave enough in the face of events.

If courage is not combined with justness, it is only a matter of bloodlust; if you cultivate this, you'll only be stronger and more perverse, without any morals. You'll therefore race to gain and flee from loss without any conscience at all. You can be exploited by authority and power but are unreliable in difficulty and danger. If people are like this, how are they better than tigers or wolves?

Tiger and wolves are by nature fierce and strong; when there is a plague, they enter towns and feed on humans, running off to nooks in the mountains where no one dares to get near them. Everyone fears the threat of wild beasts, but when they've been trapped and their claws removed and their legs tied, following along when called, running when commanded, begging food from humans, they are no different from cats and dogs. If those who are knights have no justness and no intelligence, in their lowliness they can hardly be different from these animals even if they have guts.

NINE

MURO NAOKIYO (1658–1734)

Distinguished as a brilliant student from childhood, Muro Naokiyo entered service to a lord at the age of fifteen. The lord recognized his talent and sent him to Kyoto, the ancient imperial capital, for advanced studies. In 1711 he was drafted by the central government to become a state scholar. He eventually rose to the rank of attendant lecturer and consultant to Shogun Tokugawa Yoshimune (1684–1751).

Muro was an astute military scientist and produced careful analyses of the classic treatises and historical precedents of strategic warfare. His comparison of the tactics of the two Chinese masters called Sun Tzu, namely Sun Wu and Sun Bin, is exceptional among contemporary writers, as is his critique of Japanese warriors of historical renown. Muro's moral condemnation of the craft and cruelty of the celebrated warlord Toyotomi Hideyoshi is particularly outstanding, especially in portraying Hideyoshi's famed invasion of Korea as an atrocity without honor.

■ ■ ■

The Art of War of Sun Bin and Han Xin

Although there is Sun Wu's book *The Art of War,* I haven't heard of him personally deploying an army, figuring out the enemy, and winning victory. He was hired by He Lu, the King of Wu, to whom he passed on the thirteen-chapter *Art of War.* This appears in the biography of Master Sun in the *Historical Records.*

When the King of Wu defeated the powerful state of Chu to the west and occupied Ying, the capital city of Chu, with his army a threat to the other states, I wonder if this was indeed due to Sun Wu's strategy. Since the facts of the matter have not been transmitted, there is no way of knowing. After Sun Wu, it was Sun Bin and Han Xin who used Sun Wu's *Art of War* to achieve successes that were distinguished throughout the land.

Sun Bin was a descendant of Sun Wu. Transmitting his ancestor's art of war, he became the military leader for King Wey of Qi. At that time the forces of the state of Wei were surrounding Zhao, a state allied with Qi, so the King of Qi sent his general Tian Ji, accompanied by Sun Bin, to rescue Zhao.

In the past Sun Bin had studied military science together with Pang Juan, who was a general of the state of Wei. Pang Juan had been jealous of his ability, so he secretly had him invited to Wei, where they chopped off Sun Bin's feet. So now Sun Bin just sat in a chariot and directed the army.

Tian Ji said he wanted to go right to Zhao, but Sun Bin held him back. He figured that when Wei and Zhao had been attacking each other long enough, the light troops and elite soldiers of Wei would get worn out in enemy territory, while the old and weak working transport would get worn out at home. So he said that rather than go to Zhao it would be better to head for the capital city of Wei and strike it while it was vulnerable; when the men of Wei heard their own state was in danger, they'd leave Zhao and go back to save their home state. Thus in one action the siege of Zhao would be lifted and the damage could be confined to Wei.

When Sun Bin thus headed directly to the capital of Wei, the army of Wei did indeed leave Zhao to return to Wei. The army of Sun Bin met them on the way, attacked, and won a great victory. Thus while saving the state of Zhao, instead of revealing his intention of rescuing Zhao, he made it look as if they were going to attack Wei. As he pressed with intense force, taking advantage of their vulnerability, how could the army of Wei not leave Zhao to return home?

From this perspective, if you can trap others in forms and subject them to forces of impulse, not only can you control your own troops but you can also control opponents, as if they were in your grip. Sun Bin's attack on Wei to liberate Zhao indicates his expertise in form and impulse. That is why Sun Bin said that if the forms were fixed and forces controlled, liberation would naturally ensue. If you trap them in forms, enemies will be impeded by forms; if you subject them to forces of impulse, they will be impelled by those forces and lose their freedom. So it's as if they fall for your plot by themselves.

Fifteen years later, when Wei attacked Han and Han declared its emergency to Qi, Tian Ji again led an army right toward the capital city of Wei, as he had before when rescuing Zhao. Hearing of this, the Wei general Pang Juan quit Han to return home, but the Qi army had already gone past and was in front of him.

Sun Bin said to Tian Ji, "The soldiers of the Three Jins [the states of Han, Wei, and Zhao] have always been brave and fierce and consider Qi cowardly. Good warriors use their enemy's impulses, deliberately guiding those tendencies to their own advantage, drawing them into their own schemes. According to the *Art of War,* 'pursuing an advantage a hundred miles away causes a top commander to stumble.' So let Wei get arrogant and go for spoils a hundred miles away."

With this intention, the army of Qi entered the territory of Wei. The first day, they made a hundred thousand campfires. The next day, they made only fifty thousand campfires. The day after that they made thirty thousand campfires. Each day they reduced the number of campfires, leaving them in the trail of their march.

Thus as Pang Juan pursued the Qi army he was delighted to see the dwindling number of campfires: "I always knew the Qi military was cowardly—here they've been but three days in our territory and already more than half the troops have deserted! Let's pass on and overtake them!" That day he took only cavalry, leaving his infantry behind, covering two days' journey in one day.

Now Sun Bin, calculating the trip, figured Pang Juan would reach a place called Maling that evening. There were lots of steep defiles alongside Maling, where ambushers could be hidden. Thinking he could strike Pang Juan successfully there, he had a huge tree felled and stripped and wrote on it in big letters, *Pang Juan will die at this tree.* Then he chose skillful shooters and lined up ten thousand crossbows on either side of the road, having them wait in hiding, instructing them to fire all at once when they saw a torch being raised in the night.

As it turned out, Pang Juan did in fact come to that felled tree after nightfall. Puzzled by the writing on the bare wood, he held up a torch to cast light on it. Before he could finish reading what was written, ten thousand crossbows fired at once. The Wei force was routed, and Pang Juan committed suicide, decapitating himself.

When Pang Juan had gotten Sun Bin's feet cut off years before, he didn't know that to cut off someone else's feet is to cut off your own head. One is reminded of Master Zeng's saying, "Be cautious, be careful—what comes from you returns to you." But the sayings of sages and savants must be mistaken sometimes. This must be considered an admonition for small people.

> One's feet were cut off
> So he'd never stand up in the world;
> The other may not have lost his feet,
> But his head was taken.

This is a joke of mine. If he kept his head in exchange for his feet, I'd say Sun Bin got a bargain.

Anyway, the show of dwindling campfires and the sign on the stripped tree both trapped the enemy in a form. If the campfires were seen to be dwindling, the enemy would surely follow the trail; if a sign were on a stripped tree, it was certain the enemy would hold up a torch to see. When the torch was raised, myriad crossbows would fire at once, and the enemy would kill himself. Every step took advantage of the force of the enemy's impulses.

How could this be done without figuring out the enemy and becoming familiar with the enemy's forms and impulses? After Sun Wu, Sun Bin could be said to be the only one.

Coming to the beginning of the Han dynasty (206 B.C.E.), among the generals of the founder of the dynasty it was Han Xin who was expert in military techniques and skilled in combat. The story of how he defeated King Xie of Zhao using a battle formation backing on a body of water is now known throughout the land.

According to *The Art of War*, mountains and high ground should be kept to your right and your back, while water and wetlands should be kept to your front and your left. This is the norm for military formations. Nevertheless, an army has no fixed configuration, changing according to the opponent, so there cannot be any fixed military formation.

At this time the Zhao army boasted of two hundred thousand men, while the Han army was but several tens of thousands at most, and moreover had no will to rally for a decisive battle. Because of this, Han Xin had the Han troops take up positions with their backs to water. To position a battle formation with your back to water is a deadly situation. Since they'd be driven into the water and drown if they retreated a single step, they naturally had to make every effort in a death-defying attack, having no choice but to fight.

Han Xin figured that when the Zhao army saw the Han army in a deadly situation, it would assume the Han were unprepared and would rush into combat. Then, if he had troops who'd fight to the death strike a rushing army, he'd surely gain victory in a single battle.

As it turned out, his calculation was accurate. Even so, when he had them take a stand with their backs to water, at the time the commanders may have verbally assented but they didn't agree at heart. And I imagine the enemy watching this must have gotten quite a laugh. The fact is that both enemies and allies were trapped in forms and carried away by impulse, without realizing it themselves. Even the winners apparently didn't know how they'd won.

Han Xin also used tactics such as abandoning banners and drums to feign flight, thus causing the enemy to leave their stronghold to pursue the advantage; and capturing the Zhao flag and setting up the red standard of Han to dispirit the Zhao army. In each case, as he trapped enemies in forms and used natural impulses to drive them, his allies fought all the more courageously while his enemies had all they could do to save themselves from dying.

After Sun Bin, Han Xin was the one who was expert in the formation and impulsion of military forces and highly skilled in combat. He himself discoursed upon the ability to command an army, asserting the more the better. Indeed, so it seems. Thus if we consider Sun Wu's text in terms of the arts of war of Sun Bin and Han Xin, they tally exactly. By this we can be all the more certain that the art of war is in formation and impulsion.

Doesn't Sun Tzu say, "First be invincible, then wait for opponents to be vulnerable"? First being invincible is up to us; this means a complete and invincible formation. The vulnerability of opponents is in them; it means the momentum of impulses that cannot fail to overcome them. You load your potential into a form and settle the fight with that momentum.

When you load your potential into a form, it is as deep as an abyss, submerged like a dragon; this is what is referred to as "hiding in the depths of the earth." When you settle the fight with momentum, you go into action like a whirlwind and strike like lightning; this is what is referred to as "maneuvering above the skies." Suddenly disappearing, suddenly appearing, surprise and convention produce each other, the empty and the solid form each other, like a ring without beginning or end.

When subtlety of military method reaches this point, there is nothing more to add. The bare essential, however, is that warfare is a matter of uncanny swiftness. If you are not inconceivably quick, most of your strategies will be figured out by the enemy. Also, if you keep deployed for a long time, even the commanders get bored, so where are the formation of the army and the momentum of the troops to be used? In Sun Tzu too it says, "I have heard of military actions that were crude but quick, whereas I've never seen one that was skillful yet took a long time." A good commander of armies, if he just understands form and momentum, may not know other things irrelevant to chances of victory or defeat, but for this very reason his victories are quick. This is called being crude but quick. Military scientists esteem this.

If you don't know how to calculate victory and defeat but just prepare garrisons and camps, making a complicated system of commands, planning for too long a stay, even though your military order seems completely organized without any gaps, if a military operation goes on too long changes occur, so in the end you may be defeated. This is called being skillful but taking too long. Military scientists despise this. Indeed, if warfare goes on for a long time without cease, in the meantime it uses up a lot of resources and kills many people, leaving no little long-term damage to the country.

In ancient times, when the first ruler of Shu attacked Wu, taking the role of general himself, he made a network of seven hundred camps and set up thirty garrisons, holding Wu in a stalemate for as long as half a year. This is called being skillful but going on too long. Eventually the army of Shu got tired and lost its will, and thus was defeated.

In our country too, in recent times the two tigers Uesugi and Takeda carried on a contest for superiority. It's not that either of them was unfamiliar with methods of attack, and it's not that their armies were not highly disciplined, but they didn't know how to make themselves invincible first and then await vulnerability in the opponent. With each of them trying to win a decisive victory in a single battle, they kept clashing again and again for years. This can also be called being skillful but going on too long. Ultimately nothing was achieved but the end of their lives and the extinction of their domains.

Toyotomi Hideyoshi, however, although he was inhumane and didn't make war to punish the violent and stop disorder, because he understood the major calculations of victory and defeat, would launch military expeditions without effort, deploying his troops without any clever planning. When it came to combat, he would always succeed in a single onslaught. I've never heard of his taking time off from warfare. He was close to those who though unskilled are quick. His tactics as a commander may have been beyond Uesugi Kenshin and Takeda Shingen, but as a hasty, crafty, and cruel man, he couldn't even dream of manners, music, kindness, and love. So in his later years he raised an army without honor and invaded Korea; as he kept the troops in the field for a long time and massacred the populace, the hearts of everyone in the world turned against him. This too was a disaster resulting from prolonging warfare without cease. This saying of Sun Wu's may be deemed to have captured the essence of warfare.

Warfare Is a Path of Deception

Warfare is not the normal course for sages. It might be called an expedient means. Unless you have expedient means to establish justice, warfare is a difficult path to pursue. In any case, it must be understood that warfare is something distinct, not the normal course of action.

There are differences and similarities between military forms past and present. Since the era of the Warring States the technique of figuring out opponents to win victories has been called warfare, but the same word is originally used for armed men, that is to say, soldiers. In ancient times Xun Kuang defined soldiers in terms of five types: the humane and just, the disciplined and orderly, elite warriors, brave soldiers, and skilled attackers.

The army of a king, based on principles and virtues, values humaneness and justice, so the soldiers combine their strength with hearts united, responding to the troubles of their lord like sons and younger brothers safeguarding their fathers and elder brothers, like hands and arms shielding head and eyes. This is called an army of humanity and justice.

The armies of King Huan and King Wen were faithful and dutiful, obeyed laws and rules, and feared authority so much that not a single man overstepped discipline or duty. This is called an army of discipline and order.

The army of Qin simply made rewards and punishments strict and prized the taking of heads. They knew nothing of discipline and order in the army, but they encouraged the soldiers and extolled bravery, so they liked to go to enemies and fight to the death. They were much stronger than the armies of Wei and Qi.

The army of Wei enlisted brave and strong soldiers, while the army of Qi selected men with the ability to strike skillfully.

They were assembled temporarily to fight enemies; their troops only wanted to profit, so they had no thought of fighting to the death. From this point of view, from the level of elite warriors on down there may be some qualitative differences, but all of them just grab for victory by the use of armed force, entirely ignorant of the existence of the art of war.

The art of war should be placed above an army of discipline and order. Even with an army of humanity and justice, since no army can dispense with formation and momentum, intelligence and strategy, how could you figure out enemies and win victories without them? Originally an army of humanity and justice would not get involved in complicated tricks like latter-day armies, which value deceptive contrivances and the use of double agents, but would just meet enemies head-on, either blunting their force or striking them when they slackened, or taking them by surprise or pressing them into narrow straits. Anyhow, to use strategy to control enemies without being controlled by enemies, to maneuver enemies without being maneuvered by them, is the art of war.

In one of the wars of the Song dynasty, a certain general was defending a city under siege in hot weather. The enemy repeatedly attempted to induce the defenders to fight, but the general kept the city tightly closed and didn't send out any troops. He had one man stand outdoors wearing armor; as time passed, it became hot as fire under the armor, and when the man could hardly tolerate it any longer, the general figured the enemy must be worn out by then, so he came out and rushed upon them decisively, whereat the enemy, unable to endure any longer, suffered defeat.

Even Confucius said that if you're going to mobilize military forces, you should ally with those who are wary in face of events and succeed by good strategy.

Leaving aside the affairs of other countries, distant as they are, ever since our country has been ruled by military clans, everyone has labored at aggression, so there has been no end of warfare. Since 1334 the aristocrats and military clans have been divided in the provinces, battling day and night, but all of them have collected temporary conscripts from the provinces, striving for superiority in numbers and strength of arms without any planning, pitting armies against each other like a wrestling match, doing nothing but deciding temporary victories, sometimes winning and sometimes losing, with both victory and defeat a short-lived affair, killing large numbers of soldiers for nothing. What art of war can you say there is in this? They were like the so-called clever assailants and brave soldiers.

In the twilight of the Ashikaga era, outstanding stalwarts rose up and carved out spheres of influence in the four quarters, maintaining armies of trained warriors who were always with them in action and therefore brave and strong, unbroken in a hundred battles. They might be called elite knights. Among them, the armies of Takeda and Uesugi were well organized and deployed in an orderly manner, so they would be closer to the classic concept of the army of discipline and order.

Anyway, it is at this point that the art of war can be discussed in relation to warfare in this country. Nevertheless, contemporary military scientists mostly hand on only their army regulations and don't know that the art of war is in figuring out the enemy and planning strategy to ensure victory. Those among them who are particularly ignorant of principle fortify the military by the claim that this is also the way to govern a country.

Last year someone said that according to a certain military scientist, Sun Tzu's saying that "war is a path of deception" should be read to say, "In war, deception too is the Way," not that war is a path of subterfuge.

I laughed when I heard this. It seems he doesn't like the statement that war is a path of deception and says instead that war is the straight way all along, so at times deception too is the Way.

The Chinese character for deception is read the same way in Japanese as characters for falsehood and artifice, but there are distinctions in meaning. A course of action that is not one's real motive, one that deviates from normal, is called a path of deception. So doesn't even Master Sun say, "Be competent but give them the impression you are incompetent; when deploying, make it appear that you are not deploying." If you are competent and show it, if you deploy and let your deployment be seen, how can you figure out the enemy to ensure victory?

So it can be said that warfare is a course of action that is not the real motive and that is practiced differently from normal rules. It should not be immediately identified as a path of falsehood and artifice. When you nevertheless normalize this rationalization today, you become like a hunter trying to outfox his prey, inevitably falling into falsehood and artifice.

Sun Wu, being the brilliant man he was, saw this point clearly and stipulated at the very beginning of his book that war is a path of deception. Being a path of subterfuge, it is not a normal course. If it is not a normal course, how can it constitute a way of governing a nation, especially since what has come down to contemporary military scientists is nothing but derivative matters of war, no more than capturing castles, or equipping armies, or discussing the histories of ancient wars!

People rarely read Master Sun's book, and even if some do read it they're so illiterate they don't even understand the expression "path of deception," so how can they grasp Master Sun's deeper meaning? So as I hear their doctrines, they are mostly contradictory subjective opinions, which I would say are ignorant misconstructions.

[TEN]

YAMAMOTO TSUNETOMO (1659–1719)

Yamamoto Tsunetomo was employed in the service of a lord from his youth, and wanted to commit suicide on the death of his lord, according to an ancient samurai custom. He was prevented from doing so, however, by a new law prohibiting the practice of oibara, *disembowelment of retainers on the death of their lord. Instead of suicide, therefore, Yamamoto became a Buddhist monk, which was a form of symbolic and social death. Nonetheless, like others who similarly exploited Buddhist orders for personal and secular ends, his writing demonstrates considerable contempt for Buddhism as he conceived it. His musings were supposed to be kept secret but were eventually published as the* Hagakure.

■ ■ ■

Although it's nothing out of the ordinary that warriors should keep the warrior's way in mind, everyone seems to be negligent. The reason I say this is that when you ask them how they understand the essential idea of the way of the warrior, hardly anyone can answer at once. That's because they haven't got presence of mind. So it's obvious they don't keep the warrior's way in mind. That is utter negligence.

―――

I have discovered that bushido is the business of dying. It is simply a matter of settling on dying any moment in a life-or-death situation. There are no other details. It is going forward with a calm and steady heart. To say that if you don't succeed you die a dog's death is highfalutin Kyoto-style bushido. In a life-or-death situation, you can't make sure you'll succeed.

We humans prefer to live. To a great extent, reason will take to preference. If you miss your mark yet live, you're spineless. This is a dangerous situation. If you miss your mark and die, it's death to no avail, or madness. It is no shame. This is strength in the warrior's way. When you die anew every morning and every night, becoming permanently dead while alive, you attain freedom in the warrior's way and can do your professional work successfully without blundering the rest of your life.

There are people who are born quick-witted and people who need to take time to think. Examining the root of this, even though there are differences in the level of inborn intelligence, when you think impersonally in light of the Four Vows, inconceivable wisdom appears:

1. Don't be outdone in bushido
2. Be useful to your lord
3. Be filial to your parents
4. Have the compassion to help others

You'd suppose everyone could think of profound things if they thought deeply, but they think based on themselves, so it's all stuff that turns bad by the action of perverted intelligence. The conditioning of ignorant people is such that it's hard to become unselfish. Even so, when something comes up, if you first set the matter aside, bring the Four Vows to mind, and strive to eliminate selfishness, you shouldn't err much.

Tannen Osho always said that a monk may be compassionate externally but cannot attain buddhahood without storing courage within. A warrior is brave outwardly but cannot accomplish the work of his caste without gut-wrenching compassion in his heart. Because of this, monks seek courage in the company of warriors, while warriors seek compassion from monks.

In my years of pilgrimage, I never learned anything useful for practice from Buddhist teachers. Therefore, whenever I'd hear of a courageous knight, I went regardless of the hardships of the road to hear talk of the warrior's way; it sure seems to me that it has been this that has been a help on the Buddhist path.

First off, warriors can plunge into enemy battle lines, albeit fortified by bearing arms. If monks were to plunge into the midst of spears and swords with but a rosary, what could they accomplish with only gentility and compassion? Without immense courage, they could not plunge in. As proof of that, on occasions of major ceremonies, the monks who burn incense tremble. That's because they lack courage. Kicking down dead men and reviving and rescuing beings from hells are acts of courage. But monks these days all cling to what does not exist, wanting to be pious and meek; no one attains enlightenment. What is more, they urge Buddhism on warriors, making them cowards, a regrettable phenomenon.

For young samurai, listening to Buddhism is very wrong. That's because things become two-sided. Unless you're totally focused in one direction, you won't be of any use. Elderly retirees may listen to Buddhism as a hobby, but warriors carry loyalty and filial piety on one shoulder and courage and compassion on the other shoulder; as long as they bear these charges twenty-four hours a day, even to the point where they cut into their shoulders, then samurai can do their duty. At morning and evening rites, and always when sitting and reclining, they should chant, "Lord, Lord!" That's no different from a buddha-name or a mantra. Also, they should always keep company with their clan deities. That makes for good luck. Still, examples of the annihilation of warriors with only courage and no compassion are evident throughout history.

———

Everything should be done for the sake of your lord, or your father, or for the people, or for your posterity. This is great compassion. Cunning and courage that come from compassion are the real thing.

———

The nation does not belong to one man alone; for him to see to the security and peace of all the people, and consider public servants sincerely, ought to be the root of long-term survival. If you become absorbed in governing, everything will be an aspect of government. Because the ruler's mind is the mind of his myriad subjects, it seems that it should be evident that it's ultimately a matter of his conduct and attitude.

———

It seems the nation is kept orderly by means of compassion. Wisdom and courage that come from compassion will be great wisdom and great courage.

ELEVEN

IZAWA NAGAHIDE (ACTIVE CA. 1711–1732)

Izawa Nagahide was a hereditary retainer of a feudal lord in Kyushu. He was an expert in both Japanese studies (kokugaku) and Chinese studies (kangaku) and was a prolific author. While he was overtly averse to certain aspects of Buddhism, as were many latter-day Shinto and Confucian authors, nevertheless his work contains elemental principles of Zen and Taoism in nonsectarian psychological terms. He was an outstanding thinker and wrote many books on military and political science, manners and morals, history, philosophy, and linguistics.

■ ■ ■

The origin of the warrior goes back to the divine age of antiquity when the central ruler of heaven, the Great Goddess Lighting the Sky, made a pact with her august descendant Ninigi-no-Mikoto, saying, "Let the emperor use artful subtlety like the curve of the sacred gem to govern the earthly administration; use clarity like the sacred mirror to oversee the mountains and rivers, seas and plains; and wield the sacred sword to pacify the earth and benefit the populace."

The sacred gem symbolizes flexibility and accommodation. The government of the earth should be carried out with the warm, rich quality of humaneness represented by this object. Artful subtlety is expressed by its rounded curvature; the path is not a single fixed straight line but adopts what is suitable to the time, in accord with the context. So it is a way of adapting to the time.

The sacred mirror symbolizes honesty. A mirror doesn't retain anything but reflects everything impartially, so right and wrong and good and bad features all show. Virtue is to respond sensitively to those features. This is the basis of honesty. For a mirror the essential feature is clarity. When the essence of mind is clear, compassion and decisiveness are therein. If observed with honest intelligence clear as a mirror, there will be no one corrupt at court and no savant neglected in the countryside. With the operation of government honest, and good communication between superior and subordinates, all people will find their places.

The sacred sword symbolizes decisiveness. It implies the imperative to take the side of absolute firmness and freedom from greed to destroy the internal mental enemies selfishness and treachery and execute the external bandits crime and violence, being straightforward and uncorrupted in body and mind and government affairs as well, imbued with the commanding presence to overawe the world.

If there is no accommodation, the people will be alienated, so it is good to be flexible. In the absence of dignity, subordinates will be contemptuous, so it is good to be firm. If you are desirous, your instructions won't be carried out, so it is good to be honest. Without being like this it is impossible to govern oneself, order the home, rule the country, and pacify the world.

In high antiquity there was no writing, so these three articles were made as lessons for the imperial descendants, that if they preserved the three virtues symbolized by the sacred objects, they would flourish as eternally as heaven and earth.

After this, when the imperial descendant came down from heaven, he was attended by twenty-five armed men of the celestial *Mononobe* warriors. After emperor Jimmu's expedition east, Umashimaji-no-Mikoto, son of Nigihayahi-no-Mikoto [ancestral deity of the Mononobe], because of his outstanding military achievement, was commanded to guard the imperial palace with a contingent of soldiers. His charge was called the Mononobe, or Armorer's Guild. This is how warriors came to be called *mononou*.

———

Warriors ought to keep their bravery inside, not showing it outwardly. This can be attained spontaneously after you've studied both culture and arms. In the case of those who concentrate only on the way of the warrior, however, when too young to have tempered their mental arts, if they keep their bravery inside it will invariably manifest outwardly. Like an old adage says, "With pearls hidden in it, the river is beautiful; with jade concealed in it, the mountain is lustrous." There's a type who misperceives them as weak or capricious.

There are also immoral people who are violent and vicious by nature. Everyone should be instructed after his words and deeds have been tested.

As we see current customs, people who are gentle and kindly are soft and weak, while those who are brave and bold are coarse and violent. Because of this, they should first be taught to read and become acquainted with the Way, and then taught martial arts after that. When you study in this manner, the two corruptions of soft weakness and coarse violence will not exist.

———

Once you have learned a little bit of commonplace martial arts, if you've always got a glare in your eyes, on the lookout to take others to task for what they say, even in casual encounters, you've been invaded by bloodlust and forgotten the principles of loyalty and respect for parents. Preferably you should keep boldness and ferocity inside, outwardly appearing gentle and loving.

When facing a situation where you might die, however, you should be the first to volunteer and never retreat a single step. There are situations when it's right to die, though, and situations where you shouldn't die. To die where you should die is praised as a righteous death. To die where you shouldn't die is disparaged as a dog's death.

————————

Even if you give the appearance of gentility as recommended, don't let your heart be soft and weak. Those whose appearance is gentle and who are also soft and weak at heart are what are commonly called sissy samurai. As a proverb says, "While there are no mannish women, there are many womanish men." Those who are like this are useless.

————————

When people get generally depressed, it's a common convention to say it's all up to divine decree, but that is wrong. Divine decree is in oneself, not outside. Only after you've exhausted human effort should you leave things to the divine. Consider the ancient saying "Where human effort comes to an end, *there* lies Fate."

————————

When people criticize someone else, don't join them. Lin Hejing said, "Even if you've heard it, don't say it unless you've seen it with your own eyes." As a homely proverb says, "Others' lies become your lies."

Vulgar people don't like to praise goodness; they like to expose badness. For this reason, as they go around gossiping they exaggerate one into ten, and ten into a hundred. When one person says something false, myriad people pass it on as truth. When wrongly recorded in books without resolving contradictions and left to later generations, this confuses right and wrong, false and true. We must be very careful.

Accordingly, we have to compare carefully what we hear from others. As it is said, "Listening only to one side creates prejudice." Vulgar people say good is bad if it doesn't suit them, and they say bad is good. Since they speak subjectively, they're often way off.

———

You shouldn't show any sign of making a distinction between good and bad people. But even if you harmonize, don't be influenced. If you don't harmonize, you're turning against people; if you're not influenced, you don't lose the Way.

———

It is essential that the mind circulate throughout the body continuously and ceaselessly. Where it's stagnant is called dead matter. This is what is commonly called being stuck.

———

The mind, going along with the body, should make armor go along with the body. Don't make the body go along with the armor.

———

Getting the jump on an opponent does not refer to technique. It is not a matter of attacking, nor of awaiting. It refers to the energetic state.

———

A common saying has it that the spirit dwells in an honest head. Comparing this to martial arts, in our hearts there is a broad plain called the High Plain of Heaven. On that plain we lodge our own spirit. We appeal to this spirit to remove the pollution of falsehood, bring pure light, judge right and wrong, distinguish good and evil. Standing stolidly, calm and unmoving, straight from head to hips without a slouch, mind's eye open, unblinking, may be compared to the principle of the spirit dwelling in an honest head.

————

According to an old saying, "When you open your eyes, right away you're wrong." This refers to sticking to what you see. For example, when you look to the left you forget the right, and when you look to the right you forget the left. If you look at an opponent's hands, your mind inclines to the hands; if you look at his feet, your mind inclines to the feet. Once there's any imbalance, you're like an empty house. If thieves break into an empty house, since the owner's not home he can't stop them. For this reason, you should have an overall perspective, not a biased view.

————

You should detach from arts when you have mastered them. If you do not detach from arts, you are not an artist.

————

You should fight like hitting water with a stone, not like hitting stone with stone. Hitting water with stone means using your energetic state to overpower and inhibit your opponent. Hitting stone with stone means both you and your opponent act out equally. To seek victory after having matched positions like this is either stupidity or delusion.

————

The principle that flexibility can overcome hardness should be understood. If you are adamant about being strong, that may make you weak instead. If you act strong, your opponent acts strong too.

————

The principle of the contest is to control others and not be controlled by others. Filling your body with the energy of bravery, go forth with your mind's eye open. If you go to an encounter in a calm, unshakable state, you naturally won't fall apart.

Among the vulgar are those who use sword technique to show off to people. They say the founder of their sword technique, so-and-so, made a pilgrimage to some shrine and prayed for artistry, and the spirit appeared and transmitted it to him. Or some say they learned it in a dream vision or that they attained the art of the sword by studying Zen. And some say they learned it from a goblin on some mountain. These are all big lies.

The meaning of spirit is the quality of enlightenment. When the heart is truthful, the spirit shrine inside the heart opens up at once, realized in oneself alone. A spirit doesn't come from a shrine; were it to manifest a form, it would not be a spirit but a sprite.

It is also wrong to speak of having attained the art of the sword by studying Zen. You'd have to say that Zen students also have sword teachers.

As for goblins, they are animals. What is lacking in humanity, the most intelligent of creatures, that we should learn from the likes of goblins and were-cats? Although the right way is transmitted from human to human, there's nothing unusual about that, so people concoct such things to fool people and make money. This is extremely repugnant.

———

The commonplace idea that your moves should be swift as a bird in flight is ignorant of the logic of fighting. You get like this when you're being maneuvered around by your opponent. Ideally you should move calmly and surely, threatening your opponent, keeping him hopping. This is maneuvering another without being maneuvered by the other. Rather than hop about like a bird, it's better not to miss others' moves.

However, you should concentrate on getting position. You should maneuver your opponent into a confined space, not letting him get on high ground.

[TWELVE]

YAMAMOTO UJIHIDE (n.d.)

Nothing seems to be known of this individual. His work is rather reminiscent of the writings of the immortal Chinese strategist and statesman Zhuge Liang, who is often cited by bushido writers, particularly in his grasp of human psychology and its role in the science of leadership. The material translated here was printed in 1718.

■ ■ ■

Discourtesies on the part of a general:

1. Resting before the troops do
2. Eating before the troops do
3. Taking steep mountain paths on horseback
4. Being inconsiderate of the troops' fatigue

Five disgraces for a general:

1. Too much subjective thinking without finding out the judgments of officers and soldiers
2. Arousing doubts in officers and soldiers by being untrue, saying too much so that everything is confused
3. Being inhumane, not caring about the officers and soldiers, not rewarding achievement, not appreciating effort

4. Being soft and weak at heart and not understanding life and death
5. Failing to exert effective authority, having an unfair system of laws

The three signs of a great general:

1. Always having a good reputation for knighthood among all ranks, in one's own homeland and abroad as well
2. Employing people skillfully
3. Perceiving people accurately and understanding them, putting them in appropriate posts, rewarding them well according to the quality of their loyalty and service

When the chief commander has doubts, the officers and soldiers have doubts. For this reason, when plans are settled, the hearts of the officers and soldiers are focused and strong.

It is most important to observe the hardships of the officers and soldiers and not forget them. The season is not as significant as the advantage of the ground; the advantage of the ground is not as significant as the harmony of the personnel; the harmony of the personnel is not as significant as the strategy of the general; the strategy of the general is not as significant as riding on momentum.

It is a disgrace for a general to abandon hostages in order to escape his own death. It is a disgrace for a warrior to give up on the future of the ruler to reserve his own life for his own ambitions.

It is said that the plans of the ruler should not be discussed at home. In particular, wives, concubines, and servants are weak, so if you open your thoughts to them it will be useless to regret it in retrospect.

One who does not mention mistakes of his lord, father, or teachers to people of other houses is loyal and faithful.

Not directing foul speech at enemies is an ancient principle of courtesy, even for the lowliest soldiers.

The Three Treasures are the farmers, the artisans, and the merchants. The Three Strategies are tactics, intelligence, and planning. The Four Doors of martial arts, according to Takeda Shingen, are archery, riflery, horsemanship, and military science. The Five Enemies are obstinacy, weakness, dissoluteness, pliancy, and dependency.

When brothers avenge their parents, the elder brother should make the first strike, then the younger brother should deliver the fatal thrust.

Unreasonably aggressive argument is a go-between of trouble, something sophisticated people do not like. Someone said, "Roughness is a manifestation of cowardice, a short temper is a sign of immaturity. Consideration is the ABC of prudence, tolerance is the beginning of loyalty and respect for parents, intention is the foundation of achievement."

A general of old, climbing onto high ground, saw a rainbow. Delighted, he said to his troops, "This rainbow is the energy of a cloud of defeat hanging over our enemy. If we attack tonight we'll win." As it turned out, they did fight that night and won a victory. Then there was a man named Yamamoto Kansuke in the inner circle of Takeda Shingen who is supposed to have won battles by knowing the significance of the stars.

In both cases, they saw that their chances in battle were good and used these devices to encourage their cohorts. Another went before deities with lots and prayed, "If You grant us victory in this battle, show it by the sign of 3." Then he drew lots three times, and got the number 3 each time. Seeing this, the soldiers were relieved of doubt and actually won the battle that day. What the commander had done was to discard the lots with 1 and 2 beforehand, so that only lots with the number 3 remained.

In order to encourage his troops, Di Renjie of the Tang dynasty secretly counterfeited a coin with heads on both sides, then when he'd get set up for battle he'd say to the soldiers, "If we're going to win this battle, the coin should come up heads." Then he'd flip the coin. Seeing it always come up heads, the troops thought it was supernatural and fought their way to an overwhelming victory.

All of these were strategies for settling the minds of the soldiers. It is also said that in olden times they'd designate seats of the firm and the timid every day to inspire the officers and soldiers.

Generally speaking, past and present, those who esteem boldness and power inevitably perish, while those who value humanity and justice are invariably loyal. So it is normal for a warrior to disregard his life for justice and fight to the death to be honorable.

While it is said that there is no medicine for cowardice, to die for gratitude, to die for justice, to die for power, to die for hatred, and to die for profit are all disregard for life.

Generally speaking, to be perceptive about people is most important for a samurai. You should pay very close attention to people of renown, both rivals and allies. In particular, you should always figure out who is good and who is bad.

Nevertheless, you shouldn't raise other's wrongs without understanding yourself, so you should make it a priority to do your own work well first. You shouldn't just take notice of other people's right and wrong, praising and censuring them. After all, sometimes people who ordinarily seem good may be outrageous when something happens, and there have been those who usually seem inept but perform splendidly in emergencies. So it's hard to generalize.

It is said that people who practice arts should first straighten their waist and keep their minds below their navel. Yet if you try to put your mind below your navel, your mind then stays there and can't operate. When the mind stays in one place, there's no function anywhere else. When the mind isn't put anywhere, it fills everywhere. With your mind innocent of feeling or thought, you just use your hands when you need them and use your feet when you need them. This resembles the ultimate sense of the art of war, a form of mindfulness.

There is no limit to this principle. As your art matures, you attain the subtleties. Studying carefully, thinking deeply, understanding thoroughly, when actual practice matures you naturally attain consummate accord of actuality with principle.

[THIRTEEN]

HAKUIN EKAKU (1686–1769)

Hakuin Ekaku was from a samurai family but became a Zen monk early in life and spent many years wrestling with Zen koans. In his twenties he suffered a severe mental and physical breakdown, attributed to overexertion on koan contemplation. His Zen teacher's practice of beating him up appears to have contributed to his illness, and he evidently did the same to his own disciples. According to his account, detailed in his writings but also popularized in the best-selling Extraordinary People of Recent Times, *he recovered from this breakdown by means of Taoist healing methods that he learned from a hermit. This is the source of the concentration device described in the selection translated here, from a letter of advice to a samurai. Eventually Hakuin became a famous Zen teacher, but his writing and his school retained characteristics of military training, marked by mental and physical violence.*

■ ■ ■

Instructions to a Samurai

Even if wonderful things like sudden enlightenment or immediate illumination could happen by sitting as if dead in silent awareness, still the lords, grandees, knights, and common people have all sorts of public duties and family affairs to attend to—where can they find even a little free time to sit? Even if you take time off from your job and leave household duties undone on the pretext of illness, then shut yourself in a room for three, five, or seven days with a pile of cushions and a stick of incense to sit; you'll be so tired from your everyday worldly duties that for every inch you sit you'll sleep ten feet, and in every three cups of sitting meditation you'll collect ten million bushels of wandering thought. Now if you glare and grit your teeth, clench your fists and straighten your spine and sit, all sorts of hallucinations will crowd your head.

At this point, with furrowed brow you find yourself weeping, "Official duties obstruct spiritual practice. A career in service interferes with meditation. It would be better to retire from office and go to some quiet uninhabited place by a river or in a forest, in order to practice meditation at will and escape a perpetual cycle of misery." This is very much mistaken.

Generally speaking, being someone's subject means eating food that belongs to your lord, wearing clothes that belong to your lord, and carrying swords that belong to your lord. Even water is not brought from elsewhere. You eat without farming, dress without weaving—your body, hands and feet, hair, nails, and teeth are all products of your lord's benevolence. Having thus grown up to reach the age of thirty or forty, a time when you should be assisting your lord's administration, concentrating on bringing out the ability to assist a ruler, making your lord into a lord like Yao and Shun, making the people a people like Yao's and Shun's, intent upon repaying your debt to your lord, instead you secretly finger prayer beads in your sleeve, mumble incantations to yourself, show up late for work, slack off on the job, and you may even claim illness and retire with no thought of repaying your debt to your lord.

With will and behavior like this, even if you spent three to five years in retreat practicing austerities, it might seem as if your ideas had ended and your thoughts had stopped, but your guts will be frazzled and your mind will be fearful. Even the sound of a rat crapping will make your chest seem to burst.

Whether a commander or a common soldier, in a national emergency, when it is imperative to take charge in some way, if you get people like this to secure a door in danger, when they see and hear the enemy troops rising like the tide, banners like clouds overhead, guns booming like thunder, bugles blasting loud enough to make the mountains crumble, swords drawn in rows like icicles, then they won't be able to swallow, they'll tremble all over, unable even to hold the reins, clinging flat to the saddle, shaking so hard they're about to fall. As a result, they'll be captured by foot soldiers. Why are they like this? Simply because of the three to five years of dead sitting in silence. Even a brave man would quiver if he had done this kind of practice.

——————

If you think dead sitting in silent awareness is enough, you'll waste your life and deviate greatly from the way of enlightenment. Not only will you deviate from the way of enlightenment, you'll neglect worldly truth too. Why? If the lords and grandees gave up government to sit deathlike in silent awareness, if the warriors ignored archery and horsemanship and forgot martial arts to sit deathlike in silent awareness, if the merchants closed up shop and broke their abacuses to sit deathlike in silent awareness, if the farmers threw down their plows and hoes and stopped tilling and weeding to sit deathlike in silent awareness, if carpenters discarded their plumb lines and tossed away their planes to sit deathlike in silent awareness, the nation would wither, the people would weary, robbers would rise up repeatedly, and the state would be in peril. Then the people would say indignantly that Zen is extremely inauspicious.

——————

There are two kinds of selflessness. Suppose there is someone who is always timid and weak in body and mind, afraid of everyone, mortifying his feelings so that in dealing with myriad situations he does not become angry when hollered at, doesn't mind if he's beaten, is always absentminded and doesn't learn from experience, but he thinks he has attained selflessness and considers that sufficient. This is being a broken rice bag, a fat-bellied pig in the mud, as if entirely ignorant and void of intelligence. It is not true selflessness.

———

If you always have your mental energy filling your navel sphere, ocean of energy, elixir field, and the space between your waist and legs, and you do not let it recede for a moment even when you are busy working or meeting guests, then basic energy will naturally fill the elixir field, and the lower abdomen will be slightly rounded like an unribbed ball.

If people can cultivate this state, they can sit all day without tiring, recite all day without wearying, write all day without fatigue, speak all day without getting worn out. Even if they do myriad good deeds day in and day out, they never show any sign of flagging. The mind becomes broader, the heart becomes bigger, energy is always vigorous. Even in the hottest summer one does not sweat, even without using a fan; even on the coldest winter night one does not need to wear socks or use a warmer. Even if one lives to be a hundred years old, one's teeth will become even firmer. If one does not slack off, one attains long life.

———

There are three places in the body that are elixir fields. What I refer to as the elixir field is the lower elixir field. The ocean of energy and the elixir field are both below the navel, as if they were one reality with two names. The elixir field is two inches below the navel, the energy ocean an inch and a half. When pure energy always fills here, body and mind are always equanimous. Even if you live to be a hundred years old, your hair won't thin and your teeth won't loosen. Your vision will get clearer and clearer and your skin will gradually become lustrous.

———

Spirit is like the ruler, vitality is like the ministers, and energy is like the people. Now then, caring for the people is the means of keeping the country intact. To be sparing of your energy is the means of keeping your body intact. When the people flee, the country perishes; when energy runs out, the body dies. For this reason, a sage ruler always focuses his mind below, while a mediocre ruler always indulges his heart on high. When the heart is indulged on high, the nobles rely on personal favor, the officials are arrogant with power; they never pay attention to hardship among the people, while importunate ministers greedily skim and cruel officers deprive by deception. There may be plenty of vegetables in the fields, yet people are collapsing from starvation in the countryside. The intelligent and the good go into hiding, ministers and commoners are angry and resentful, the masses of people are ultimately reduced to abject misery, and so the pulse of the nation dies out forever.

When the mind is focused below, never forgetting the toil of the people, the populace is well nourished and the state is strong; no ministers or commoners violate the law, while no enemy states invade the domain. So it is with the human body. The perfect people always have mental energy filling below, so the emotions do not act within, while the material world cannot invade from without. With the camp guard fully supplied, the mental spirit is strong. Ultimately the body doesn't know the sting of acupuncture or moxabustion, just as the people of a powerful nation don't hear cries of alarm.

[FOURTEEN]

HOJO CHIKUHO-SHI (SEVENTEENTH CENTURY)

The identity of this man is unclear, but one theory is that he was Hojo Ujinaga, a famous military scientist, or a follower of Hojo's school. Hojo Ujinaga (1609–1670) was a direct retainer to the house of Tokugawa, the Shoguns of the Edo or Tokugawa period. He is known to have authored several books totaling nearly ninety volumes, and he was the martial arts teacher of the famous Yamaga Soko, who has been called the virtual founder of bushido as a systematic philosophy. His school, called the Kansuke school after the master Yamamoto Kansuke (1501–1561), is also called the Takeda school because one of its famous graduates was the undefeated warlord Takeda Shingen (1521–1573). The date of the source of the selections translated here, Instructions for the Way of the Knight, *could be 1747 or 1687. The linguistic forms suggest the earlier date of composition.*

■ ■ ■

The Path of the Knight

The path of the knight is martial. Leadership by principle is cultural, leadership by punishment is martial. Management of the ordinary is cultural, management of disturbance is martial.

Even so, martial means are not something devised and applied when disturbance occurs. Since disturbance occurs within order, lack of constant martial preparedness produces disastrous disorder. So when a ruler does not cultivate virtue, does not educate the people, and does not amount to a protector, then the civilians drift away.

As long as knights are not competent in the warrior's way, knights too are vagrants.

The Rules of Knights

A basic text says that there are many rules for knights, but essentially there are no more than three. Those three are planning, intelligence, and strategy. These are the three essentials for inside, outside, and emergencies.

Internal order is called planning, knowledge of the outside is called intelligence, and calculation for emergencies is called strategy.

These all involve mind, body, and phenomena, essentials that no one, from ruler, commander, and knight down to ordinary men and foot soldiers, can ever depart from, whether in normal times or in emergencies.

The Body of the Knight

Awesome courage and firm strength constitute the body. Master Zeng said, "A knight has to be strong." Our country was governed by aristocrats in ancient times, but because their bodies became soft and weak there was no end of disorder in society. After them, since Minamoto Yoritomo, government has been run by warriors, so fear of strength and ferocity quelled rebellious ambitions in society. Is this not submission to martial authority?

As I see the samurai of the present time, from the lords and grandees down to the soldiers, under the benevolent rule of peacetime they are becoming like aristocrats and women. Unable to stand up to a strong wind, keeping their hands and feet soft, on top of that forgetting the ways of warriors even in their minds, absorbed only in the comforts of the present, they leave the fate of their own country, even the management of their households, to educated employees, doing as they like, mindless of resentments in the home or misery among the farmers, just acting as they please.

Samurai are originally born into the caste in charge of killing and attack, so their hands and feet should be hardy, making nothing of mountains, rivers, and seas. They should train their bodies in cold and heat, night and day, so as to become strong in every way. But samurai today—lords, commanders, and officers alike—are pale of face, the soles of their feet are soft, they wear socks and caps. Their form may be that of samurai but their bodies are like aristocrats and their hearts are like women.

How perilous! This should be well understood. The body should be strong, the heart robust.

The Service of Knights

Sobriety is considered service. There are, however, differences in service in normal times and in times of instability. Service under normal conditions is done by way of straightforwardness, service under conditions of instability is done by way of subterfuge.

Yet people don't understand the Way or the service of the knight, and their application is also incorrect in normalcy and instability, as they mix them together and use subterfuge for everything. Misunderstanding this as the Way of the knight is a fundamental error.

Sun Tzu said, "Warfare is a path of subterfuge." The path spoken of there is not the Way we refer to as the warrior's Way. How could there be error in the Way? That is why Sun Tzu specifies warfare, meaning that when it comes to war, subterfuge is the way.

War is an emergency. Once it comes to combat, facing a contest for supremacy, you can't win by such seemingly praiseworthy sentiments as the true way being humanity and justice, the humane having no enemies, and so on. If the humanity and justice of the royal way were intact, then there wouldn't be any warfare, only orderly peace according to the teachings of sages.

In latter days, however, people's hearts are not honest, and the ways of ruler and subject, father and son, elder and younger brother, and friend and colleague have all changed. In abnormal times, how is it possible to govern but in the martial way? When the world is orderly, keeping to the Way of sages, the exceptions of subterfuge need not set the tongues of military theorists wagging.

Also, the saying that the humane have no enemies is like the charisma of a great king; it refers to having already become personally humane. Nowadays there is only the theory of being humane; no one is really humane. Therefore, in times of disaster and disorder, when it comes to controlling abnormalities, how can the job be done without subterfuge?

Ignorant people who are unfamiliar with the art of war but have heard fragments of classics think that artifice is sinister and want to imitate the way sages and savants govern in times of normalcy. They enunciate various different doctrines, but doesn't this amount to artifice in respect to the way of warfare? This is not Sun Tzu's intention.

Even so, if you think that subterfuge is the whole of the warrior's way and make use of subterfuge in the context of normal political and social relations, this too is a big mistake. Subterfuge is used against enemies, like weaponry. Why would you use weapons against your allies?

It is also very much mistaken to understand intelligence, strategy, and planning as subterfuge. Planning, intelligence, and strategy are essential basics, all of which are required in dealing with everything, whether directly or by subterfuge.

Let everyone understand: it is in order to correct injustice and effect rectitude and justice that knights temporarily employ subterfuge to subdue people and govern the land and the nation. Therefore artifice is employed for the sake of correction; artifice is not used for the sake of deception. Those who use artifice well gain the straight way; those who master subterfuge to do what is right gain the nation. Those who know what is right but don't master subterfuge lose the nation.

The Methods of Warriors

The methods of warriors refers to military science, the principles of warfare. In combat there are differences between attack and defense; differences in the terrain of mountain and river, sea and land, forest and plain; and differences in size, strength, and cunning of the enemy. There are principles of combat according to these various differences, but in any case it is hardly possible to win without mastering method. Those who know will win; those who don't know will lose.

When you are victorious, you establish yourself, revive the nation, and distinguish your name in the world. When you are defeated you kill yourself, lose the nation, and sully your name to posterity. This is because of not knowing the appropriate methods.

Today, however, things change from time to time between ruler and subject, father and son, husband and wife, elder and younger brother—if you don't recognize these changes and respond to developments according to the situation, dealing with people skillfully, whether by being proactive or by exercising restraint, thus harmonizing them, then political and social relations will be disorderly. Then how can the governance of the changes of the day manage to master the methods of dealing with the major disruptions of war?

The Humaneness of the Knight

For a knight, reward and punishment constitute the art of humaneness. This does not refer to the common conception of being like a woman or a girl emotionally, not even killing a bug, letting beggars and outcastes take things, feebly being kindly to good and bad alike, not executing those who deserve to be executed, not prosecuting those who warrant prosecution.

For knights, the practice of humaneness is summed up in defining rewards and punishments to encourage good and reprove the bad. For example, when one man acts in a perverse way for which myriad people suffer, by executing that one villain you gladden the hearts of all the people, and by punishing one criminal you teach a lot of people a lesson, changing the attitude of the masses. When someone does good, you reward it to make the people envious and thus encourage them to good ways. This is making everyone good—is that not great humaneness?

The Heart of a Warrior

The key to the warrior's heart is maintaining courage. Courage means your mind and your mood do not get upset or lose normalcy. This is called being stalwart.

So the commonplace conception of courage as simply being unafraid when seeing or hearing frightening things is not complete courage. When neither normalcy nor emergency moves your mind, nor even sensual desires, when your expression doesn't change even if a mountain crumbles before you, you don't get angry even if people offend and insult you, you aren't fazed even by a major war, you're unafraid even when death is imminent, your heart is not discouraged by poverty and loss, you are not intimidated by people in high ranks and high offices, your mind is not distracted by trifles, you are not scared of anything, and you are unfailingly fearless and imperturbable, this manliness is called courage.

FIFTEEN

TAKAYAMA KENTEI (fl. ca. 1761–1764)

*Nothing much is known of Takayama Kentei except that he was at one time
a consultant to a feudal lord. The advice translated here, originally written
for that lord, presents a wide-ranging summary of traditional political and
military science, deftly combining Shinto, Taoist, Legalist, and Confucian
concepts of society, government, and warfare.*

■ ■ ■

Keys to Order and Disorder in the History of Japan

Foundations of Order

An old classic says, "The light of the deity of the sun illumines
all things. When people follow that light, the country is orderly;
when people turn away from that light, the country perishes."

To govern a country, why use foreign laws? When we stand
on the natural state of our country, whatever comes we adapt it
for our use, so why reject foreign laws?

It's just that when the relation between the fundamental and
the incidental is lost, it is impossible to effect complete order
in the country. This is where the keys to the science of government come from. If those who are interested in this science
would quiet their minds and perceive the natural state of the
country, what would be hard about securing the whole land?

1. *The Substance of the Nation*
After heaven and earth separated, myriad countries were divided. This was due to the evolution of invisible matter. The invisible extending to all countries is called correctness. To attain correctness and manifest the natural state is called virtue.

Because of the natural state of Creation, countries are inherently different physically, and people's dispositions are different. The country of Japan was governed and pacified from the first by bravery and strength. This is termed martial; it is the disposition of our country bestowed by Creation.

To govern a country by expression of its disposition is called knowing the substance of the nation. Those who do not distinguish the substance of the nation but try to govern it by alien doctrines are very mistaken. The foundation of the great science of governing is in understanding the substance of the nation.

2. *Beginnings*
In the beginning of countries, humans and animals were indistinguishable. Intelligent humans, using knowledge of nature, invented food, clothing, and dwellings. It was by imitating them that the majority of humans, who had no foresight, first began to prepare meals, cover their bodies, and shelter from rain and snow. By following the intelligent, they were able to survive, so they accepted their direction spontaneously, thus distinguishing the positions of leader and followers.

Fathers and mothers produce children, whom they care for because of their flesh-and-blood relation, and who respect them as parents on account of this care. Thus love and gratitude between parents and children comes about naturally.

From this, social norms are defined; from this, classes and ranks are established. Only the person at the top, wishing to stand by the natural destiny of the multitude, teaches and guides them to know their stations, using a uniform law to enable everyone to make a living.

In later ages, various principles were expounded, but nothing beyond the state at the beginning of the country. People whose eyes are open to this should not find it hard to stabilize the country and renew its order even in later generations.

3. Maintaining Order

Our ancestors founded the nation, issued laws, established education, and nurtured the masses of people. Later generations, as their descendants, find it hard to cause the country to follow. As time passes, what was formerly considered right may become wrong, while what was considered wrong may now be right.

If we just attend to establishing the laws and norms of past ages while seeing to the welfare of the masses, enabling them to find their places according to the times, not using our personal subjectivity, we should not corrupt social order or destabilize the nation.

4. Equilibrium

A country has myriad people and myriad things, all existing naturally and all performing some function for the country. When people are out of place, they injure each other and rob each other. When things are out of place, they lose their function and become waste.

How could this be natural? If we were like the spring breeze and the spring rain, who would not benefit? If we were like mighty rivers coursing over the earth, where would we fail to reach? Even if alien teachings rise like sword points, they all become ours. This is something that ought to be seen.

5. Selective Appointment

The affairs of a nation are multifarious. Even if there is an enlightened commander on top, it is impossible to comprehend everything within the seas by means of the knowledge of one individual. Therefore we select intelligent people and give them offices and assign them jobs according to their abilities.

With this, the ministers of state devote their intelligence and energy to their tasks, benefiting the nation. When the ruler effects supreme order without lifting a finger, it is by appointing the intelligent.

When you take pains with selection, appointment is easy. When you make selections in a principled way, apart from subjective likes and dislikes, people will not be able to conceal their good and bad qualities. When you appoint them and do not doubt them, people do their best. For the art of government to extend throughout the land is a matter of appropriate selection for appointment.

6. Communication and Blockage

Perpetual undisturbed order in a nation depends on the communication of human feelings between above and below. When human feelings are communicated well, everything flows smoothly accordingly and could not be thrown into disarray even if you tried.

When a nation is always agitated and disorderly, it is because human feelings above and below are blocked. When human feelings are blocked, everything is suffocated and could not be put in order even if you tried.

The order or disorder of a nation is most of all a question of circulation or blockage. When those above are not out of place and those below do their work diligently, then human feelings are communicated spontaneously. When those above cannot manage their position and those below neglect their work, suddenly human feelings are blocked.

It is imperative to decide whether to rely on principle or stick to subjectivity.

7. Provincial Characteristics

Countries differ in size, terrain, climate, accessibility, and fertility of soil. The warmth or coldness of people, the withering or ripening of grains, the presence or absence of fish, salt, flax, and mulberry, the utility of the woods and metals, all produce some benefit for the nation, according to their provincial characteristics. There is no greater art of government than discerning this.

8. Provincial Customs

Governing a nation is principally a matter of governing people. Governing people is in knowing their dispositions. Knowing their dispositions is in distinguishing provincial customs.

Humans are the most intelligent of beings. Though the people of all nations are not different, according to the provincial characteristics of the places they were born their temperaments are not the same. Becoming habitual, they differ in their strengths and weaknesses.

When you distinguish their differences accurately and make use of their strengths without attacking their shortcomings, people are all useful to the nation. If you neglect their strengths because you hate their shortcomings, then people do harm to the nation instead.

Distinguishing provincial customs is key to governing people. Their natures, moreover, are not more than five types. If you are familiar with the fundamentals, how would you lose people?

9. Human Feelings

Joy, anger, sorrow, happiness, love, hatred, desire—these are the seven emotions of human beings. They are phenomena that become active when the mind contacts objects. Human sentience depends on their existence, and so does human evildoing.

Because people are physically different, the way they are affected by things also differs from individual to individual. For example, when you observe a group of people, you find that some are pleased, some are angry, some are sad, some are happy. There's no uniformity. If you don't make them the same, you cannot govern.

Generally, when people have something to rely on, even their feelings easily unite. When they lose what they rely on, even mutually sympathetic people go their own ways. When a single aim is established, some stick to it angrily, some stick to it gladly, some stick to it sadly, some stick to it happily. Their feelings are quite different, but what they rely on is the same.

Knowing people's feelings is a deep secret of the art of government. It requires examination.

10. The Power of the Earth
Supporting myriad beings without wearing thin is the virtue of the earth; fostering the growth of myriad beings in their naturally ordained state is the merit of the earth. When man stands between heaven and earth and does his best with things on earth according to the order of heaven, the power of earth should manifest naturally.

Governing the country and settling all people in their places is possible because of the things on earth. Only in places where human knowledge hasn't reached or the earth is not fully utilized is its efficacy not seen.

Even if you have colossal strength you cannot obtain crops from a soil that won't produce them, like looking for fish in the mountains or trees in the sea. Where there is a state, there are people, and there are all sorts of things. For the produce of the state to support its people is the natural order. If the produce of the land cannot support the people, produce of other lands is sought to sustain them, ultimately leading to famine. This is due to failure to fully utilize the land.

When they recognize what is there and what is not, and they grow what will grow in abundance, then the various states will naturally trade what they have for what they don't, so there will be no shortages. The basis of enriching the country is all in this.

11. Training and Discipline

Enabling people to do their jobs is training; coordinating people to carry out the functions of a state is discipline.

People aren't born with knowledge; only when the mind is corrected and vigor expands through work is one able to fulfill one's own function.

Even if each individual masters his own work, if the whole society is not coordinated it is impossible to function as a state or protect security.

To have the warriors practice martial arts and the farmers work at tilling and production is training. For those of the knightly caste not to lose their proper places, following the leader as one, getting the people of each farming district and village to collaborate and provide mutual assistance, is discipline.

In governing people, to enable them to perform their functions, nothing is beyond training and discipline.

12. Taxation

There is disturbance and tranquillity in a state; you stand by leading the people in both conditions. To let the people keep their produce in times of tranquillity, while seeing to it that people don't lose their way in times of disturbance, depends on proper taxation.

When foodstuffs and military equipment are enough for the number of soldiers a state has, so that it is not adversely affected

by disturbances, this is because of attention to military operations. The rule is that the grain exacted according to the popu-
lation of a state, minus the cost of transport, is to suffice state
needs, while the proper measure is that the people can live on
what's left.

If calculations are accurate, then there should be no loss of
normalcy on account of disturbance or tranquillity.

13. Economy

There are years of abundance and years of scarcity; there are
tragic events and auspicious events. When you govern a mass of
people, if there is no surplus in normal times, you cannot help
people out in emergencies.

Events are manifold; if you don't pay attention, the needs
of the country cannot be met even in normal times, much less
emergencies. Calculating income, you make expenditures.
When you add up all needs, you should know whether you'll
have a surplus.

Not to do what ought to be done is stinginess; how can that preserve the country? Doing what shouldn't be done is extravagance;
how can that support the people and save them from famine?

When you do what should be done and don't do what
shouldn't be done, the country has a surplus even without
expecting it. This is the secret of economy.

14. Success and Failure

Among the many things you have to deal with in governing a
country, some things are bound to succeed, while some things
are bound to fail. When you don't discern what is succeeding
and don't pay attention to what is failing, this can build up to
cause harm to the country.

When your mind is on the Way, you do what is likely to succeed, and prevent failure; because of this the country is orderly. When your mind is drawn by feelings, even if you know something should succeed you can't do it, and even if you know something is going to fail you can't prevent it; because of this, the country comes to ruin.

Someone who is expert at understanding potentials for success and failure can go to any country and govern.

15. Discerning Potential

What has sprouted can be seen and discerned by everyone. What has not sprouted, not everyone can see. Trying to respond to things once they've become evident is like trying to overtake a racehorse with a mule. It's too late to be effective. When you perceive things before they've sprouted, you're ready to deal with them before they happen. Then when the time comes you respond like water putting out fire. Your work all goes as planned.

Order is potential chaos, plenty is potential paucity, life is potential death. Is it far off? Everything around you is potential.

16. Perpetuity

Don't think total order is achieved in one generation. When the blessings of benevolence flow downward generation after generation, supreme order comes about naturally. The Way can perpetuate; clever contrivances invariably fall short.

Correcting yourself, you respond to what comes. It's not that you seek others, but they come and join you. If those who would govern well are ignorant of this, no matter what they may do they cannot govern the country in perpetuity.

17. Temporary Measures

Administrative affairs are complicated, with infinite variations. If you are not a man of great measure, you will not be able to deal with them effectively. If you try to decide every matter that comes up according to a single rule, those matters will be delayed and neglected, and those concerned will feel suppressed. But if you detach from opinion and keep things in perspective, forget your own effort and consider others' peace of mind, matters will get straightened out as you take them up, like untangling threads with a comb.

The perpetual is the constant, the temporary is the expedient. If the constant is not well established, there's no use for expedients. If you don't know expedients, the constant cannot be responsive to actualities.

18. Laws and Regulations

There are myriad beings between heaven and earth. Creatures without intelligence stand on the natural order mindlessly; humans have minds, so we cannot stand on the natural order because we have thought.

A human ruler governs in place of the divine. What causes all people to stick to their natural standing is called law. What establishes people in their proper places according to the times is called regulation. What is established in perpetuity is law; what is established for a particular time is regulation.

The compass and rule of political science must be understood.

19. Reward and Punishment

A country has important laws that keep people in their proper places. Nevertheless, people are living things; when they're idle they break laws, and when they're desperate they violate laws. The only thing that keeps those laws intact is proper reward and punishment.

It is not a matter of giving rewards out of fondness or administering punishment out of dislike. Those who abide by the law and are beneficial to the country you reward for the sake of the nation. Those who violate the law and harm the country you punish for the sake of the nation.

This way everyone will act according to the law, fearing to break the law, and the law will stand unopposed. Then the nation would not be disorderly even if you wanted it so.

Independence

Even if a ruler is an expert in the principles of government, when he himself is not upright, how can he run the administration and govern the country and the people? Yet if you only try to make yourself upright and don't attain expertise in the principles of government, you don't escape self-righteousness.

An ancient classic says, "As humans have a soul, when they thoughtfully rely on principle, its light illumines the world, but when they thoughtlessly indulge in feelings, the darkness destroys the person." When you rely on principle, your mind naturally is not fixated on the physical body; when you transcend yourself for the nation, myriad virtues naturally appear.

If rulers are ignorant of this, how can they govern well? How can they deal with disorder and subdue rebellion? Should we not be careful?

1. Reality and Falsehood

The pure essence of something is called the reality; loss of the pure essence is called falsehood. Humans are the most intelligent of beings; if they stand on earth obedient to the divine order, they manifest the virtues of heaven, earth, and humanity. Nurturing all beings on behalf of heaven and earth can be called fulfilling that essence. This is due to the virtues of enlightened commanders merging with heaven and earth; their intelligence is brilliant.

When people cannot follow the divine order and do not stand in their own proper places but compete with each other, violating the principles of heaven and earth, losing their intelligence by their intellect, it is because ignorant commanders are drawn away from principles by feelings.

If commanders who would lead the nation and educate and nurture the people don't open their eyes to this, even if they come up with millions of ideas it will be useless labor.

2. *Impartiality and Selfishness*

Sharing happiness with everyone else is called impartiality; indifference to everyone else's sorrow is called selfishness. When you rely on principle for the sake of the people of the nation, everything is naturally impartial. When you covet things for your own sake, all is inherently selfishness.

A ruler is like the sky. Everyone can see whether the sky is dark or light, but no one praises or blames the sky for darkness or light, because the sky has no bias. When a ruler reigns without understanding this state, whatever he does is selfish; how can he protect the country and govern the people?

3. *Reason and Principle*

If you have any doubt or misgivings about anything in the world, you should not occupy the position of leadership for even one day. To have no doubt whatever about anything in the country, seeing everything as clearly as looking at the palm of your hand, is due to mastery of reason and principle.

The pattern of nature is called reason. When you see through that pattern, there is no difference in the root of heaven, earth, and all things—what is there to doubt, what is there to be apprehensive about?

For everything to abide by that reason is called principle.

While all things differ, everything naturally has its own pattern. Everything flourishes and is useful to the nation when it is well established in its pattern. How can a commander lead the nation without seeing through these two things?

4. Justice

Heaven nurtures all beings without bias, because its mercy is perfect, fundamentally free of love or hatred. A ruler's relation to the multitude of people below is like heaven covering everything, leaving nothing out, because of the impartiality of heaven.

If your standpoint is not upright, you cannot deal without everyone impartially.

Therefore distinguishing what is to be done from what is not to be done and standing by what is right is called justice. There is no better way for a ruler to reign over subjects than by justice.

5. Self-Sacrifice

Buddhists talk about self-sacrifice, but don't rely on their interpretation. A ruler's relation to his nation is to govern all beings in place of the divine; if his mind is on his body, he cannot stand in that position. When he keeps wholeheartedly to principle and takes responsibility for the welfare of the nation and the people, he has no time to think of the pain or pleasure of his body. Because his mind is not drawn by his body, his feelings are naturally right. As long as he does his duties in the right spirit, he will not lose the rank of rule.

6. Frugality and Measure

Ornamentation invites extravagance, simplicity naturally produces frugality. When people are essentially pure and simple, they naturally don't do what they shouldn't.

Here is where a leader should stand. But there are higher and lower ranks; when you lose your rank you become stingy, so not to deviate from one's position is called measure.

With frugality as the basis, when you don't lose measure your situation is inherently correct. When you make division of ranks principal, you forget frugality. Then you'll drift into extravagance and won't know how to get back.

7. *Familiarity and Distance*

When in charge of a nation, you draw close to the wise and distance yourself from the unworthy. From the viewpoint of social norms, you are close to relatives and distant from strangers.

The political standpoint is public; familiarity and distance depend on worthiness or unworthiness. The personal perspective is private; familiarity and distance are matters of identification and otherness.

The world is not one man's world, it is the whole world's world. For rulers to draw close to savants and distance themselves from the unworthy is a uniquely essential aim.

8. *Labor and Leisure*

When people labor, they do not depart from principles. When at leisure, they stray from principles. That is a natural pattern.

All humans of all classes have both labor and leisure. Wise commanders belabor their minds, while their bodies are at ease; stalwart soldiers belabor their bodies, and their minds are spontaneously at ease.

If those on top belabor their bodies, the government offices will be empty. If those on top leave their minds at leisure, the nation will lose its order. The proper places of labor and leisure have to be distinguished.

9. Different Inclinations

People's hearts are not the same, just like their faces. As their thoughts are different, so are their inclinations. You want to get all the people in the land, with all of their different inclinations, to head in one direction. It seems like forcing the impossible. But approving the good in people's hearts and disapproving the bad is the same for all.

When you don't force this with what is different but invite what is the same to induce people to abide by principles, then before long they will love each other and assist each other. This is a key secret of governing people.

10. Appointing People

Smart people like everything to come from themselves, while stupid people are comfortable when everything is directed by others.

There are limits to human intelligence, while the affairs of the world are infinite. To attempt to handle limitless affairs of a nation with limited knowledge is really due to lack of attention to principle.

A ruler's relationship to his ministers is like that of a master carpenter to his tools. The design of a building is done by the carpenter's knowledge, but the work depends on the employment of tools. The government of a country is the potency of the ruler, but the work is done by the efforts of the ministers.

So a master carpenter chooses his tools. When a master commander chooses his ministers to put in office, delegating duties to them without doubting, keeping the peace within the seas is as easy as turning over your hand.

11. Humility toward Others

Even an intelligent person cannot avoid one mistake in a thousand thoughts, while an ignoramus may spontaneously get it right once in a thousand thoughts.

Governing a country is a matter of governing the people. Winning the people is a matter of knowing their strengths. Knowing their strengths is a matter of being able to be humble toward others.

Words of country folk become standards of nations; housewives' sayings become models for myriad ages. If people have abilities, take them at their abilities, not their words; if people speak well, take the sayings without demanding proof.

When rulers can be humble to others while remaining in their position, they make the knowledge of the whole land their own knowledge. There is no greater knowledge than this.

12. *Admitting Criticism*
Wood is made straight by compass and square; people keep their places because of criticism. When listening to the affairs of the world with the ears of one individual, there is nothing like criticism.

When a ruler knows that criticism is a good thing but cannot listen to criticism, so there is no one to criticize him even if he wants criticism, it is because he does not open the way for it. If you try to listen selectively to pleasant words, you can't find it anywhere. By choosing good words, you make known your dislike for unpleasant words, so ministers think they can't speak out.

Whenever you want to open the way for criticism, it is a matter of admitting a wide range of opinions, emptying yourself to listen to them. When you do not decline even random criticisms, then accurate criticism will come even without being sought. When you admit accurate criticism and change the errors of your ways, then everyone will spontaneously submit. No medicine compares to this for a ruler to preserve his state.

Responding to Disturbances

An ancient classic says, "If you make sun and moon your banners, with thunder and lightning your troops, the soldiers of rebel armies will stretch out their necks for the sword." If you do not distinguish the unjust from the just, whom to kill and whom to let live, you cannot master the arms of the Divine Warrior.

The military of our country esteems extreme yang and forbids yin subtlety. It is beyond the schemes of sundry military scientists. Being yang, it is able to correct; being correct, it moves well. Therefore when it meets unjust armies who concoct treacherous strategies, it fights them to the finish like boulders rolling over eggs, crushing them, unstoppable.

It is important to realize the mysterious skill of a spiritual army.

1. Potential Disorder

Potential may be immediate or delayed. When the east wind rises and rain starts to fall, this is an example of immediate potential. The first signs of a scorching summer appear the previous winter; this is an example of delayed potential.

Although there are differences in immediacy and delay, potential is no different. There is disturbance within order, and there is disturbance within chaos. If you don't perceive their potentials, you cannot deal with disorder so as to keep the territory whole.

2. The Times

If you arbitrarily plan for the present by means of knowledge of the past, your affairs will not proceed. If you know the present but not the past, your work will be in vain. If you intend to rescue the people on behalf of heaven, there is sudden takeover, there is independent achievement, there is a time to wait and watch for opportunities.

One who thoroughly understands the times is considered a good commander. One who is ignorant of the times is called an ignorant commander. This is the essential handle to dealing with disturbance.

3. *Organization of Things*
A battlefield may be an abnormal situation, but the things involved are all everyday things. If you always keep things well organized so they are not out of order, then their uses are evident. If everything in the country is organized so that it can answer properly to emergencies, then there's nothing to fear from myriad enemies.

4. *Observation of Things*
When you're going to do battle, how can you win victory if you don't discern where the enemy is vulnerable and where the enemy is solid? Before fighting you should have people find out the enemy's vulnerability or solidity.

The time of year, the pattern of the terrain, the forms of preparations, encampments, castles, forts, cavalry, infantry, javelins, instruments of killing force—all of these are things. You should see those things, no matter what they're called, seeing with your eyes until you can see with your mind, hearing with your ears until you can hear with your mind.

This way you'll penetrate all vulnerability and solidity, internal and external.

5. *Moving an Army*
Leading an army to a distant enemy land is something that has always been considered difficult, throughout history. When people are in the mood, they'll willingly go a thousand miles; when they're not in the mood, they'll scarcely go a mile.

Troops get in the mood to go by aiming for success; what would be hard about leading those who want to go? There are bridges and boats for river and sea, paths can be cleared through the mountains. Nevertheless, without the fighting spirit, what will they do even if they go? In a pinch, they'll snap at once.

Therefore, if you develop people's spirit so that they are as if seeing the enemy close at hand, then the lines of march, security watch, and signal systems will naturally get organized, and there will be no worry that people won't be amenable to instruction.

6. Encampment

When you take advantage of the energy of momentum, you can crush enemies. Where the energy of momentum is inhibited, you scatter in defeat.

All human energies are nurtured by rest, yet they are also sapped by rest. That is why the organization of a camp has always been considered an important element of a contest. Supporting the spunk of the troops so they can be deployed at will is in the critical issue of the method of encampment.

Supply routes and terrain are fundamental to cultivation of momentum and energy. The structure of the encampment is to facilitate transport and deployment. Although there are many tasks involved, when you control the keys you should be able to keep a tight camp under your jurisdiction.

7. Forms of Preparation

Even if you have a million men, how can they be adequate to fight when endangered by enemies? When you lead a group to take on enemies from all sides and not get thwarted in combat, this can be called good preparation.

As to the forms, the preparations of expert commanders have always been a topic of discussion by military scientists of all times. Even if you are familiar with all the precedents, what use is that?

Generally speaking, preparations are like water. Water takes on forms according to the container. Its main characteristic is simply to flow downward. Preparations have no form; they take on form according to the terrain. Their main point is to defeat enemies. If you penetrate this, infinite forms will be at your command.

8. Castles and Forts

A castle is where all things circulate, where a ruler protects the territory. Therefore organizing a castle is like running a household. The rule for a house is to serve ordinary purposes and to respond to emergencies. The general outline of a castle is no more than this.

When attackers' weapons fail, it is because of the security of the castle. No one can see in from outside, but you can see everything; no one can come in from outside, but you can go out. When you're on the defense, enemies don't know where to attack; when you go out to fight, enemies lose their defensive positions. The advantages in conflict are such that you can stand up to ten times as many men.

While there are many kinds of work involved, when you design the structure without knowing what's essential, just as in house building it will naturally be ineffective in the crisis of conflict.

9. The Scale of War

There has been warfare ever since the age of the deities, generation after generation, countless times, doing no more than contending for supremacy. Nevertheless, the scale of warfare has differed from ancient times through medieval times to recent times. Weapons have gradually increased, from relatively few to very many; the scale of warfare has changed over the ages according to the performance of those weapons. This is natural.

If you don't know the differences in the scale of warfare, you cannot take charge of combat. While knowing about scale, if you lose what's most critical to war by getting stuck at a certain scale, you can't win victory that way either.

When it comes to warfare, the work of an intelligent commander is to make himself strong and invincible, be well prepared, watch enemies and strike their vulnerabilities, fierce and unrelenting. If you make this the basis for comprehending the scale of war, even though there may be all sorts of difference in forms of preparation and quantities of equipment, why worry? Use whatever is there, without any fixation.

10. Cavalry Combat

Cavalry combat is an ancient type. It provides for speed, the ability to break through defenses. You don't get stuck in battle, and it facilitates cutting across the meadows to chase down the fleeing and kill them. It is not to be used on steep and difficult terrain; it is done on level ground.

The men and the horses are products of training. Although the action is elegant, you shouldn't get so stuck on maneuvering as to miss your opportunities. Take care that you're sure what's essential.

11. Infantry Combat

Infantry combat is a close-range style. It provides for density, the ability to shut off city streets to fight it out. Infantry marches easily over grassland, keeping in order. It is useful for steep and difficult terrain, while on level ground it may have less standing. Unless you master the main tasks of stopping and starting, advancing and withdrawing, resting and mustering; the art of renewing energy; and the secret of sizing up a battleground, you cannot reach expertise in infantry combat.

12. Military Equipment

With the intensification of the scale of warfare, instruments of death increase. Basically they are not what determine victory in combat. All uses of military equipment—assisting combat, increasing the power of soldiers, facilitating their work—are accomplished by training. There is that which leads to victory depending on the distance, there is that which assists the action of the soldiers, there is that which keeps up the energy of momentum. Even if more military equipment is invented in the future, its intention cannot be any different. When the fundamentals are clear, the operation of the equipment will arrest the momentum of enemies without even trying.

13. Peasant Militia

Although offense and defense each have their own function, they are both essential to the maintenance of a state. In a contest of warring states, an enlightened commander excludes enemies from the state he holds by virtue of peasant militia.

It's not that he trains them for military service from this day forward, but he has always viewed them as if they were his children, while the people look to their leader as to a parent. When their parents' country is under enemy siege, as their children who would watch empty-handed? They go into action regardless of life or death, and that energy is enough to take away the enemy's momentum.

When teams are properly organized, groups of men work together so they can take all the necessary steps. Their wives and children are gathered together and looked after, so they don't worry about their families. When directed, they all become special forces. This is the adaptive strategy of an enlightened commander.

14. Defense and Attack

In combat there is defense and there is attack, both of which invoke potential gain and loss. Don't be eager for action. Depending on the times, there is attack and there is defense. When you properly put down rebellion, you're on the attack over ten thousand miles; when you refrain from aggressive warfare, preserving rectitude, you may have to defend against attackers from all sides. These are natural phenomena.

When you are blinded by the gain and loss of defense and attack and you lose the key of military action, then gain becomes loss. The defender, being secure, wanes in force, while the force of the attacker, who is vulnerable, soars to the skies.

Viewed in terms of form, a large army is always the attacker, while a small army is always the defender. An expert commander mostly fights aggressively, while an ignorant commander mostly fights defensively.

15. Offensive Strategy

Offensive strategy is the secret of attack. Seeing the spot and striking it intensely is the meaning of attack. It is not bloodlust. Where the spirit reaches, it will smash even through iron walls. If you don't know this state, there's no benefit in aggressive warfare.

When the action goes as intended, this is called strategic planning. Maneuvering so as to take away the enemy's momentum is offense; using tactics to break the enemy's will is strategy. First you take away the energy of momentum, then you break the cutting edge, finally you bring about complete submission. The secret of attack is no more than offensive strategy.

16. Defense and Prevention

In land combat, nothing is more important than defense and prevention. When standard equipment still functions properly in emergencies, that is the meaning of defense. To assure beforehand that you will not yield even if assailed from all sides is complete defense. Then even if enemies attack in countless different ways, you have nothing to fear.

To be ready with something suitable to strike an opening and have it at hand in emergencies, to hit enemies' vulnerabilities accurately, is the meaning of prevention. To determine where to take advantage of the enemy's vulnerabilities before they even come is adaptive prevention.

Thus you will not be forced to yield even if the enemy surrounds you with ten times your number and attacks you with five. By striking exactly where you have planned, you can put a huge enemy to flight. Nothing is more important in ground warfare than defense and prevention.

17. Night Combat

Night combat is the opposite of daytime; it is not usual. No one who is inept at daytime combat succeeds at night combat, while it is possible to be thoroughly versed in daytime combat and yet inept at night combat. That's because the times are different.

It's not that the leader of night combat depends on night. It's a matter of taking advantage of nighttime to carry out operations with uncanny swiftness, manifesting extraordinary action. Though officers and soldiers are both sure of the signals for night combat, when they're first issued they'll be as if ignorant. Even if the men are well trained, if they miss their opportunities they won't be effective.

There are always opportunities. When you yourself create the opportunities, you can strike at any time. Don't seek techniques. Where mind and spirit reach, dark night is like broad daylight.

18. Naval Combat

Naval combat is the opposite of land; it is not usual. Those inept at riding on land can hardly navigate water routes, while one may be good at land combat yet inept at naval combat. That's because what's underfoot differs.

It's not a matter of depending on boats to fight but expediting your operations by boat to show up unexpectedly and score a great success.

When you can see where you're going, that constitutes a route, whether on sea or on land. If you are definitely equipped for victory when you're going to set sail, and your spirit is conveyed to where the enemy is, you're like waves flooding the land in a hurricane.

Therefore trying to engage in combat on water by virtue of expertise in navigation is where ignorant commanders get stuck. How can they achieve the effect of uncanny swiftness?

19. Battle to the Death

Luck can run out or deliver success. Even an intelligent commander gets surrounded and runs out of tricks and tactics when his luck comes to an end. When your number is up, there's nothing you can do but honorably preserve good principles to the death.

They are wrong, we are right—how could we die at the hands of rebels without doing anything? Convey to the troops the determination to fight to the death, send the cowards away, burn the supplies and cut off the way back. When the men of all ranks are united in forgetting death and life, eager to kill even one rebel, raging into battle, aiming to kill the enemy commander, racing freely, never retreating a step, this is the action of the dutiful who are determined to fight to the death.

Without this, even an ordinary battle will be dangerous. But when you're like this, the spear point of one man can oppose several dozen men. As for the vicious blade of a desperate enemy, you may be able to destroy him easily if you sidestep his ferocious force.

20. Military Food Supplies

Warfare is a major undertaking for a nation, and the expenses of a nation at war are countless. Even with a full arsenal of weaponry, if food supplies are insufficient, both attack and defense are impossible to accomplish. So this is a foundation of defeat. Therefore an expert commander sees to it that there is a surplus of grains, in peacetime as well as wartime, to be prepared for emergencies.

Even if there's enough food for land combat, supplies can't last on an expedition. If you rely on shipping alone, once the routes are blocked the army starves. This is something that military scientists consider a problem.

Even so, the famous commanders of our Warring States era went to war year after year without running out of food. Obviously, even at the stage of aggressive warfare, unless you conquer enemy territory, how can you cross borders and advance at will?

It's not only a matter of food supplies. When beleaguered by enemies in front and behind, the army goes to death and destruction. When on the move, figure the distance; take advantage of ally territory to advance, then when you come to enemy territory attack and subdue it, and after that take the road. Wherever you go there are people, so it cannot be that there is no food— you take it all from the land, appropriating it to your own use.

Once a castle falls, then there are plenty of food supplies.

Added to that are supplies sent by allied commanders nearby in the region. And of course shipments from the home state arrive sooner or later. Then what will there be to worry about?

21. Access to Water

Water is critical on a war front. Even if there is plenty of food, if water runs out, men and horses will wear out and sicken right away.

There is drinking water, water for use, and water in reserve. If you are ignorant of these provisions, you will break down in emergencies. Even if there is water now, it may run out. Enemies may cut off access to water.

Beginning with well water, flowing water, and rainwater, if you don't make sure of provisions ahead of time according to the number of your men, you'll lose free use of water.

22. Vulnerability and Solidity

Generally speaking, vulnerability and solidity alternate endlessly and cannot be avoided by either the intelligent or the ignorant.

An intelligent commander is usually solid, but sometimes vulnerabilities occur. An ignorant commander is usually vulnerable but occasionally happens to be solid. This is why an intelligent commander normally wins battles, while an ignorant commander usually loses battles.

Vulnerability versus solidity, solidity versus vulnerability, vulnerability versus vulnerability, solidity versus solidity—if you don't have real insight into victory and defeat, you cannot tell which is which.

23. The Tide

Though vulnerability and solidity alternate, changing in a moment, when you observe them attentively you can see them clearly. Even so, it is hard to see where vulnerability becomes solidity or solidity turns to vulnerability, being so subtle. And even if you can see, if you can't respond you can't do anything about it.

To launch an action accurately on seeing the opportunity is called knowing the tide. Winning every battle is no more than a matter of knowing the tide. To win when it is easy to win and establish success in the world depends on mastering this.

24. Spiritual Force

What is inconceivably penetrating is called spiritual. What is unstoppable on the attack is called force. When your mind pierces your enemy's bones and marrow and your energy swallows armies, this is called spiritual force.

Spiritual force manifests when you can perceive victory and defeat before the fact. When you fight with spiritual force, myriad enemies cannot put up resistance; wherever you go they submit to your threat and your mercy.

25. Taking Territory

On the attack, you take enemy territory. Don't use overwhelming force but reassure the populace, bring complete order to the territory, and then move on.

When you begin to take enemy territory, if your system is just and facilitates people's livelihood, your new subjects will submit to you. As you make progress, wherever you go they'll clear the way, offer you supplies, and race to surrender.

The critical business of a just army taking territory must be penetrated clearly.

26. Restoration of Order

An enlightened commander stops rebels and enemies on behalf of the deities. Like sunshine melting frost and snow, wherever his army goes, there is reconciliation.

Once the land is pacified, what is there to do? Returning to the divinely ordained natural state, we should transmit normalcy perpetually. Good warriors have nowhere to exercise their canniness, while an unsophisticated populace enjoys its work and supports the ruler. Here is where the manifestation of the order of nature can be seen.

27. Command
From the outset of an expedition through victory in battle to return to camp, to be able to lead the troops to advance as one and withdraw as one, like the mind employing the hands and feet, not losing discipline in times of danger and stress, not diminishing in force when at rest, altogether unyielding from beginning to end, depends entirely upon correctness of command.

It is no wonder that distinguished generals of old were careful about this. When a command is established such that it is enacted from above without exception and accepted below without violation, as the men are more in awe of commands than of enemies, then all the multifarious tasks will get done, while every hidden and subtle opportunity will be discovered. For a million men to traverse the land without peril is all a matter of well-established command.

[SIXTEEN]

HAYASHI SHIHEI (1738–1793)

Hayashi Shihei was descended from a long line of hereditary knights of the Tokugawa Shogunate. He traveled all over Japan making observations on topography, local customs, and administration and became obsessed with the threat of invasion of Japan by foreign empires. As Japan was officially isolated and internally peaceful at the time, Hayashi was viewed as using sensationalism to seek fame and was censured by the Shogunate and condemned to confinement. While in confinement he sat in a single room deep in thought, it is said, never taking a single step outside until the day he died of illness. His warnings were remembered decades later when Russians plundered Japan's northern territories, and he was formally pardoned fifty years after his death.

■ ■ ■

Armament of an Ocean Nation

What is an ocean nation? It means a nation with no neighboring countries on a contiguous land mass, bordered by oceans in all four directions. This being so, for an ocean nation there are military preparations proper to an ocean country, of a different class from the doctrines of the Chinese military books and the traditions historically transmitted in Japan. Without knowing this distinction one could hardly speak of Japanese military arts.

171

First, there is a reason why it is easy for invaders to come to an ocean nation, and there is also a reason why it is hard to come.

The reason it's easy to come is that in military vessels they can travel distances of two or three hundred miles in a day or two if they get favorable winds. Because it is this easy to get here, we ought to be prepared.

Then again, the reason it's hard to get here is the perils of the ocean on all sides, which make it impossible to come at will. Even so, don't rely on that peril so much as to neglect preparedness.

In this connection it seems to me that when it comes to Japan's military preparedness, the most urgent task ought to be knowledge of a method of preventing foreign invasion.

Now then, the method of preventing foreign invasion is in water combat. The key to water combat is cannonry. The organization of these two is the proper military preparedness for Japan, different from the military systems of mountainous countries like China and Tartary. Only after having knowledge of water combat should we be concerned with land combat.

It's a pity that even the famous military men of Japan, being trained on the basis of Chinese military texts, all transmitted only Chinese military principles; no one discussed ocean nations. It's as if they knew the one but not the two. The reason I begin my discussion with water combat is that this is the basis for military preparations proper to an ocean country.

Given that Japan's primary military preparation should be for warfare on water, there is another point to be understood, and that is how ancient China and modern China differ, geographically as well as temperamentally.

The first attack on Japan from abroad ever since its founding was during the Yuan dynasty of China, which repeatedly sent military forces. In particular, in 1281 they came pressing with an enormous force, but luckily they ran into a divine wind and were all killed.

The ruler of this Yuan was a man of a northern race who had taken over China, so under the Yuan dynasty, China was consolidated with the lands of the peoples to the north, and military operations on the northern frontiers ceased. For this reason he could send troops and horses far away without worry, and that's why he sent forces against us time and again.

You can see the trend of the times in China from this. Never mind antiquity; even up to the Qin and Han dynasties, they had no precise knowledge of the size of Japan or of the sea routes. During the Tang dynasty there was frequent intercourse with Japan, so they got to know the sea routes and provinces in detail. But because of our mutual amity, they never invaded. Coming to the Song dynasty, as the ways of that dynasty were soft and weak, they couldn't come here. And the ones who destroyed the Song were the northern race of Mongols, namely the Yuan.

The reason the forces of the Yuan got to Japan, as mentioned, is that China and the territories of the northern peoples had been amalgamated, so fighting on the borders between them stopped, and therefore they could send troops far away without worry.

Subsequently the founder of the Ming dynasty destroyed the Yuan and restored China. His governance was not soft or weak, for he was able to achieve unification. In this era there was some talk of invading Japan, but because the Chinese were constantly harried by major enemies of the northern races, they had no time to come far across the sea. On top of that, when the ferocious power of Hideyoshi conquered Korea, as the Chinese were unable to attack, fleeing his momentum toward Beijing, they were destroyed by Tartars.

Since the Kangxi era (1662–1723), China and Tartary have been amalgamated; now they are even more united, and the northern borders are peaceful. Therefore they could send forces to distant places without worry. What is more, the emperors of the Kangxi, Yongzheng (1723–1735), and Qianlong (1736–1796) eras have been formidable rivals, both culturally and mili- tarily, masters of the momentum of the time, able to keep China in hand.

Don't think this is the same China as it was up to the Ming dynasty. Present-day Qing, compared with ancient China, has twice the territory. Their martial arts carry on the ways of the north, and they are well trained. Their passions have also been influenced by the northern races, inclined to hardness and forcefulness, so eventually the greedy mind-set of the people of the north gradually infested China, whose customs of humane- ness and cordiality gradually waned.

In addition, books have become more informative with every generation, and intercourse with Japan is frequent. People's minds, moreover, are becoming more aware all the time, and now in China they know Japan's sea routes and provinces in great detail. It seems to me that a future ruler of Qing, taking advantage of freedom from domestic troubles and considering the precedent of the Yuan, might do something rash.

If it comes to that, because their motive will be greed, they won't take to Japan's humane government; and since they'll rely on a massive force, they won't be scared by Japan's military threat. This is how different it is from China up to the Ming dynasty.

Also, these days the power of Muscovy in Europe is unrivaled, invading the northern lands of distant Tartary. Recently they invaded Siberia and annexed as far as Kamchatka in the farthest east. But there's no more territory to take east of Kamchatka, so I hear there is evidence that they're looking back westward again to take the Kuril Islands east of Ainu country.

Already in 1771 a character exiled by Muscovy to Kamchatka, Baron Moritz Benyovszky, had set out by ship from Kamchatka, come over to Japan, and sailed around more than half of Japan measuring the depths of the harbors in port after port. In the process, in the province of Tosa he sent a letter to a Dutchman who happened to be in Japan at the time.

The attitude underlying such events is to be hated and feared. Because this is an ocean country, we should note how ships that shouldn't be coming do in fact readily come, at the whim of the people on board.

Now that we have distinguished between the situation of an ocean nation and the trends of the times in China, there is yet another point to be understood, namely that we should aim for both cultural and military completeness, not falling into sheer militarism. Sheer militarism is barbaric; it is benighted.

Fundamentally, *weapons are instruments of ill omen.* Nevertheless, as they concern life and death, destruction or survival, nothing is more critical to the nation, so they cannot be entrusted to barbaric and benighted militarists. That is why in ancient Japan two colleges were set up in the capital, military and civil, while militias and local schools were set up in the provinces, so everyone had both literary and military education.

Confucius also expressed the idea of completeness in both culture and arms, declaring, "Those who have culture must have military preparedness." Besides him, Huang Shi wrote on how a nation should be managed both culturally and militarily, and Sima Rangju said that not forgetting war in times of peace is the way to safeguard a nation. In addition, the six nobles of Jin, Guan Zhong, the two founders of the Han dynasty, Kongming of Shu, and our divine ancestor were all men who had understood the import of both cultural and military completeness.

There have been many others who in Japan and China discoursed on warfare, but they all passed on their own particular expertise and were one-sided militarists, so they can't be called both culturally and martially complete.

When it comes to the way of waging war, moreover, each country has its style. Generally speaking, Japan's way of warring is skirmishing, mainly bloody battle with little planning, the foremost method of war being just to rely on the country's natural bravery, sacrificing one's life to destroy the enemy. Although the brunt of the attack is sharp, because the method is crude it is hard to effect a state of caution. As the Chinese respect both principle and method, strategize and plan a lot, and consider caution foremost, while their military formations are magnificent, when it comes to bloody battle they are very slow. In this connection, if you read the military histories of Japan and China, you'll recognize the swift and the slow.

There is also the example of a mere nine men from Japan, Shibuta Hachiemon, Hamada Yahei, and others, going to Taiwan in the Kan'ei era (1624–1644) and capturing a Dutch general.

Also, during the An'ei era (1772–1781), when I was working at the military headquarters of Hizen, sixty-one Chinese in the compound at Nagasaki ganged up and created a disturbance. Fifteen of us went there at the command of Security. We killed all sixty-one at once and burned down the shrine where they were holed up. Having fought a showdown with Chinese at that time, I personally experienced how slow the people of that country are in combat.

Also, the countries of Europe concentrate on firearms, heavy and light, and have very many other kinds of projectiles. The designs of their ships, in particular, are extraordinarily sophisticated, and they are expert in naval warfare. Those countries also have a religion, moreover, that keeps them orderly and on friendly terms with one another, so that countries of like persuasion don't attack one another but invade yet other continents together, striving generation after generation to make them their own possessions, with like countries never warring against like. This is something neither Japan nor China ever even attempted.

If those who lead armies can understand the conditions of these three militaries and adapt to circumstances, they can overrun the world.

To begin with, no previous Japanese military scientist has ever elucidated the implications of Japan's being an ocean nation, the peril of being negligent in view of the superiority of contemporary Qing over ancient China, and the differences in the ways that Japanese, Chinese, and Europeans wage war. The reason they haven't elucidated these three issues must be that all the military scientists have concentrated on Chinese texts, so they naturally fell into line with Chinese thinking and didn't realize that for an ocean nation there is a military system proper to an ocean nation. The reason I'm starting to talk about it is that I have a deep concern; I've asked around, thought intensely, and come up with this idea.

Even if you understand this, a normal member of society shouldn't disclose it. It shouldn't be disclosed out of prudence. I'm a simple and direct loner, so I can throw caution to the winds. Therefore, beginning with the Benyovszky case, I have written all about how easy it is for foreign invaders to come.

Combat on Water

Military preparedness for an ocean nation is at the seacoast. The art of war at the seacoast is in combat over water. The key to combat over water is cannonry. This is a natural military system for an ocean nation. That's why I raise this issue first. Be aware that there is a deep meaning to this, which cannot even be discussed on the same day as ordinary military texts.

When there is prolonged peace, people's minds relax. When people's minds relax, they forget about disruption. This is a common failure throughout history in both Japan and China. Not forgetting this is called military preparedness.

In the present day it is a common habit to think that foreign ships can enter port only at Nagasaki and no other harbor. Those who think this way can indeed be called people who drum their bellies complacently. Already in the past foreign ships have entered ports many times at Bonotsu in Satsuma, Hakata in Chikuzen, Hirato in Hizen, Hyogo in Settsu, Sakai in Izumi, Tsuruga in Echizen, and so on, presenting gifts and carrying on trade. So as I've said in the introduction, because this is an ocean nation it is possible to sail into port in any province at will. Thus even the eastern provinces cannot afford to be off guard.

Considering the matter on this basis, just as we have mounted cannonry set up at Nagasaki harbor and are in a state of readiness there, we should set up defenses like Nagasaki everywhere in Japan—east, west, north, and south. This should be the main principle of defense for an ocean nation.

Now, this is not a difficult undertaking. If we establish a new system now and gradually build up our defenses, we might expect to be able to fortify the entire coastline of Japan quite securely in fifty years. Don't doubt it—when we accomplish this, it will be like building a castle three thousand miles square called Japan, with the oceans for moats and the seacoasts for stone walls. Won't that be pleasant?

Personally, it seems very strange to me that there is heavy cannonry at Nagasaki but no such defenses at the ports of Awa and Sagami. When you consider it closely, from Nihonbashi in Edo, past China, and all the way to Holland is a borderless ocean route. So why do we have defenses only at Nagasaki and not these other harbors?

As I see it, lords ought to be established in the provinces of Awa and Sagami and heavy defenses set up surrounding the straits between them. The defense of the entire coastline of Japan should begin with this inlet mouth. This is particularly essential to the military preparedness of an ocean nation.

Even so, to tell it like it is without reserve is disrespectful. Yet not to say anything about it is disloyal. That is why this isolated individual braves punishment to write this.

Combat over water requires utmost attention to ship design, first and foremost. Next is thorough training of captains and sailors in the operation of warships. Next, all soldiers should be taught how to swim, ride a horse in water, and row. These are three essentials of combat on water.

On reflection, it occurs to me that in the three thousand years since its founding, Japan has never set up cannonry on its coasts, and yet we are still secure, even now. What is more, we've never been sorely tried by foreign invaders. So to start speaking sententiously about the defense of an ocean nation now seems overwrought, or sensationalistic, or even insane, but it is an established pattern that changes inevitably occur in everything in the world and all human affairs. Don't think it will be just like today forever!

What is more, the countries of the five continents have been civilized for as much as six thousand years or more, with even the youngest at least three thousand years old. And every country has heroic and exceptional people who have accumulated the knowledge of more than three millennia and figured out astronomy, geography, and navigation, as clearly as looking at the palms of their hands. So the heroes and characters of the five continents all aim to invade other countries far away; this has become a universal attitude these days.

This attitude is particularly abundant in the countries of Europe, in the people of the Christian nations. Even so, in order to take distant countries, they don't rush into war but just talk of gain and loss, charming the local people and only then taking over.

When you think on this basis, now Japan is a long way from Europe, and moreover it has always been our disposition not to accept what they say. It's too far away for them to attack militarily, so Europe is nothing for us to worry about. However, I've heard something privately. It has been said that in recent years some people of China-Tartary have had friendly relations with Europeans. If they get much closer, the heroes and stalwarts of China and Tartary might convert to Christianity. If they become Christian, they'll start wanting to invade and plunder.

If their ambition to invade and plunder is enough to bring them to Japan, it is close by sea, and they have an abundance of soldiers and horses. If that happens, unless we're prepared we'll be helpless.

[SEVENTEEN]

TOMIDA DAIRAI (fl. ca. 1800)

Tomida Dairai was an educator, civil administrator, and prolific writer. He had a very strong classical Confucian bent, including a decided antagonism toward Buddhism as understood in his time.

■ ■ ■

Regardless of social class, there should be no discourteous behavior.

Courtesy moderates and graces people, and should never be lacking. When you lose it, you're not even as good as an animal. This principle appears in various classics, but to start with familiar examples, suppose you ignore people on the road and pretend not to notice them because it's too much bother to greet them, or you overtake and pass someone riding, or you deliver a verbal message standing in the foyer, or you carry swords when you get out of a carriage to greet someone—there are countless such discourtesies.

As the duty of courtesy is especially important, ultimately if the grandees in charge of government are not personally correct in this respect, those of lower ranks can hardly live up to it. You should read the *Zuo Tradition of the Spring and Autumn Annals* and reflect further on this. Here I bring up one corner to get you to figure out the other three.

The virtuous shouldn't be envied; the ignorant and immature should be looked after.

If you not only fail to improve yourself but also envy others' virtues, that can be called the most ignorant ignorance there is. The crimes of libel and slander are listed as early as the *Manners of Zhou*.

Some people criticize others' studies as pedantry. Some parents even stop their children from studying, claiming that learning new things is poison. Impeded thereby, even determined people give up.

People without learning, who do not discern the Way, are as if standing with their faces to a wall, not seeing anything. Even if people like this live a long time, it's meaningless. But as long as you're of a class dedicated to service of the ruler, you cannot just do as you please and refuse whatever you don't like.

Looking after the ignorant and immature is an aim of a noble man. It is natural to consider how to encourage people in good ways and be useful to the state. Being capable, you take pity on the incapable; wanting to be established yourself, you establish others. All of this comes from sincerity.

There are many men of small measure in society who keep books hidden as rare texts, not even loaning them to others, making them food for silverfish. This is ridiculous. Not only this, but whatever is useful to people ought to be passed on and disseminated throughout society. The ambitions of small people, in any case, are merely self-serving.

Warriors should not believe in Buddhism.

If you are influenced by Buddhist doctrines such as reincarnation, you'll become weak-minded; your vigor will be drained. Also, the use of scriptural passages, Sanskrit letters, and spells on swords, armor, banners, and signals is a disgusting sight.

The doctrines of reincarnation and retribution are expedients to deceive and seduce ignorant people. For example, in the battle of Kulikala several tens of thousands of people fell dead at once, but their past sins could not have all been simultaneous. Also, in the olden days, during the era of Warring States, if you personally killed one man you'd be summarily executed as a criminal, but if you killed twenty or thirty men you'd be rewarded as a hero. And then if you killed countless people you'd become a regional lord and be flourishing in your time. If you killed even more to take the whole land, everyone within the four seas would look up to you and you'd flourish forever. There is no so-called retribution here—why is that?

In any case, a warrior should respect martial virtues and always concentrate on developing vigor. If you just use Buddhist scriptural sayings such as *Don't do anything bad, do everything good* to encourage good and discourage bad in ignorant and small people, sometimes it can be a help.

EIGHTEEN

ADACHI MASAHIRO (fl. ca. 1780–1800)

Adachi Masahiro was a martial artist and military scientist. He founded a branch of the Divine Warrior school of martial arts in Kyoto. His writing devotes a great deal of attention to psychological conditions and their outcomes in combat. While nominally Shinto in accord with the temper of the times, his school evinces characteristically Taoist and Zen elements in its tactical analyses.

■ ■ ■

Yin and Yang

Military training is yang, extremely active. The time of impending battle is extreme yin, still and quiet.

When you are extremely calm on the verge of battle, even your facial expression does not change. You don't fixate on the opponent; you don't stare the opponent in the face. You don't advance like crossing a narrow bridge but like walking down an open road.

One whose state of mind appears normal is a yin opponent. This is a superior technique, hard to oppose.

As for yang opponents, one displays rock-crushing force in his facial expression, a second embodies rage, a third tries to stare his opponent down, a fourth storms in and strikes with a loud cry, a fifth moves in and out forcefully. These are called yang opponents. The minds of yang opponents are moving, which makes them vulnerable. Nonetheless, a yin opponent may strategically become yang, so you always have to watch out.

Reality, Action, Groundwork

Groundwork means cultivating the techniques transmitted by your teacher to be able to maneuver freely, strengthen your body, and solidify your skills.

Action means knowing the underlying intent of the techniques transmitted by your teacher, mastering the principles of combat.

Reality refers to the state where you are single-minded and imperturbable after having successfully cultivated groundwork and action.

As an analogy, when a smith forges a sword, the preliminary forming of the blade is the groundwork, filing an edge on it is action, and the crossing of blades sharpened on a whetstone is reality.

One who has attained the reality, action, and groundwork is called a master.

The Physical Mind and the Basic Mind

Martial artists have a physical mind and a basic mind. The physical mind refers to knowing the principles of victory and knowing techniques but being unable to perform those techniques. The basic mind refers to mastery of the techniques and principles of victory and the ability to perform the techniques at will.

The reason the techniques that the physical mind knows don't actually work is that the mind stirs. The reason the techniques known to the basic mind work is that the mind doesn't stir.

The reason the mind stirring is called the physical mind is that when the mind is calm at a deep level it does not stir, but the mind becomes excitable when it floats uncontrolled, so when the mind is between the skin and flesh it is called the physical mind. The sense in which the mind unmoved is called the basic mind implies withdrawal of the mind from skin and flesh to settle it in the gut below the navel, unmoving—this is called the basic mind.

As an analogy, the basic mind is like eating delicious food, savoring its flavor, and swallowing it. The physical mind also eats, as it were, but the food stays in the mouth and doesn't enter the stomach. When the mind lingers between skin and flesh and cannot be controlled, it becomes confused in emergencies. The basic mind, making both principle and technique its own, being single-minded and certain, opens an eye through the navel, so it is not thrown into confusion in emergencies.

Practicing Swimming in a Dry Field

In contemporary bamboo-sword contests, even if one wins by one's wits, there are a lot of martial artists who practice swimming in a dry field. What this means is that with swords made of bamboo covered with leather you don't get hurt badly even if you're struck or stabbed, so even a physical-minded martial artist may win by his wits. When it comes to a contest with real swords that can cause fatal wounds at a touch, it's hard to get by with the wits of the physical mind. Contemporary cowardly physical-minded martial artists think they are masters if they win bamboo-sword contests with a little bit of theory. This is a big mistake. If you rest content with the small swordsmanship of bamboo-sword contests, you'll get way out of line.

In any case, you should reflect on the principles of victory in combat with real swords and train yourself to be single-minded and undisturbed even when facing a powerful opponent.

Now at the present time there is no warfare going on, so there's no trying out combat with real swords, and consequently there's no way to know how strong or weak our minds will be, or how excited or calm, where real swords are used. Nevertheless, when you train your mind under ordinary circumstances, your mind will be calm and unafraid even with real swords.

Training the mind means, first of all, solidifying courage and getting rid of timidity. Second, it means self-sacrifice. There are traditions besides these, but they cannot be known without being taught by a technician with an imperturbable mind.

Solidifying courage means going out and spending nights in places such as mountain forests, graveyards, woods and rivers, places where apparitions appear. There are traditions about this, but even if you don't know a tradition, it is worthwhile practicing. Confucius said that a noble man does not approach what is dangerous, so there may be people who think this practice goes against the Way. However, it is for escaping danger and for overcoming enemies, accomplishing great deeds, and sustaining steadfast loyalty, so it is not different from the Way of a noble man.

Anyway, though mental exercises can't be perfected without a teacher's instruction, since this writing explains the principles of mind, if you understand this writing well and always train your mind to be as is written here, this itself is mental training, so you should eventually attain an imperturbable mind.

Mental Posture

Although there are various postures in every school, such as upper, middle, and lower guard, posture is in the mind. When you are single-minded and sure as you face an opponent, that is posture.

Physical posture and sword position are of uncertain value; as you act on the moment, with nothing fixed, reacting to your opponent, the position of your sword is not to be relied upon.

Even if he builds an iron citadel and makes a secure fortress, if the commander's mental posture is bad he won't be able to hold it. When the mental posture is right, even without a secure castle there is no disorder.

Takeda Shingen held several provinces, but all of his life he used natural fastnesses for his citadel; because his mental posture was good he didn't particularly need security in a castle. Yet not only did he maintain his holdings but all of the warlords in the land feared him. Such is mental posture.

Whatever form of posture or stance you adopt, your mind should be formless.

Four Attacks

The four attacks are the direct attack, the counterattack, the changed attack, and the strategic attack.

In our school, a direct attack means when you face off with an opponent you strike him before he strikes you. A counterattack is when you deflect your opponent's attack and follow up by striking. It's called counterattack because you counter your opponent's sword blow.

A changed attack is when you have attacked with a direct strike, your opponent counterattacks you, and you strike from a different angle. A strategic attack is a tactical strike at an opponent.

A direct attack may work even without expertise, but a counterattack won't work without a considerable degree of skill and mental calm. Strategic attack is a maneuver of the resourceful.

The reason a direct attack may work even without expertise is that while victory and defeat depend on the level of training, the ease of using direct attack is that you strike first regardless of the opponent. Counterattack requires you to apply the technique on seeing the opponent's striking sword, so you can't do it if you're inexperienced. As for a changed attack, since you launch it after you fail to land a blow and your opponent counterattacks, you can't do it successfully until you've attained mastery.

Five Technicians

In our school the term *five technicians* means there are five types of martial artists: the aggressive, the clever, the technical, the calm, and the masterful.

The aggressive are those who come at opponents ferociously with overwhelming force, their minds so intent as to blast through rock. The clever mainly use their wits to strike opponents strategically. The technical are those who concentrate on winning by means of the techniques their teachers have passed on, plus the techniques they have worked out themselves. The calm concentrate on watching for an opening in an opponent's defense to strike. The masterful overcome people with the subtlety of the imperturbable mind.

Being aggressive means excessive yang, facing opponents with stone-shattering force. Warfare focuses on yin. Yang is moving, yin is still. Stillness should be the focus in warfare. When yang, the mind moves; when your mind moves, you cannot win.

The clever figure out opponents strategically with their wits because they are ignorant of the principles of victory and the techniques of winning. There are these clever ones even among the inexperienced, and also among the highly skilled, but not among the masterful.

The technical are so called because they try to win with technique. The technical are better in a way than the aggressive and the clever, because the techniques taught in the various schools are all techniques for winning. To employ the techniques taught by your teacher is the basic idea of training; using techniques you've devised yourself on top of that is knowledge.

Of course, it is hard to win by virtue of technique while you're still inexperienced. So to think the techniques transmitted by a teacher are useless is a sign of insufficient training. There are a lot of people who abandon techniques transmitted by teachers to rely on their wits, but as long as you are adequately trained, the techniques transmitted by a teacher are usable. These technicians can ultimately become highly skilled and even attain mastery.

Those who watch for opponents' openings to strike are called calm because they are technicians who have arrived at the state where the mind is quiet. To gain victory on seeing an opening in an opponent is for the skilled, impossible when inexperienced. With experience, a technician can become calm.

People who win by the subtlety of the imperturbable mind are called masterful because they have reached the ultimate attainment. A master is a technician with an imperturbable mind.

One who attains calm can become a master. While the aggressive and the clever cannot reach the state of mastery, if they realize this principle, the aggressive reform their excess and the clever realize that wits don't reach the principle of technique, so they shift their focus to technique and calmness. Then they can eventually reach the state of the supreme way.

As for the strategic attack of the clever, it's all right to strike strategically on occasion while concentrating on technique and calmness, but when technique and calmness are in order, you realize you don't need strategic attack and don't rely on it.

The excess of the aggressive is the beginning of the loss of life. One should be wary of this. But even aggressiveness is a different matter if the aggressiveness is strategic while the inner mind is still and silent. This is something done by the highly skilled among the clever.

Outward Courage and Inner Courage

There is outward courage and there is inner courage.

Outward courage shows bravery in the exterior appearance,

and in face of combat manifests the force to smash even iron and stone. In addition, one like this is normally vigorous and inclined to forcefulness, and has no regard for people. A man with the heart to tear even a wild beast apart, who appears to the eye of the ordinary person as a brave man, exemplifies outward courage.

Inner courage is courage that is not displayed outwardly but kept in the inner heart. Unlike outward courage, this does not make the face stern and solemn and is not an inclination to forcefulness or a manner of speech. It refers to courage with a gentle face but a strong root.

Outward courage is like aggressiveness, while inner courage is like calmness, or mastery. Of course, when you reach the state of mastery, you are both outwardly and inwardly courageous.

The strength of outward courage is like fire; the strength of inner courage is like water. Fire is forceful yet weak, while water is yielding yet so powerful nothing can oppose it. One with outward courage, like fire, has a weakness; one with inner courage, like water, is extremely powerful.

The courage of the common man, and the courage of bloodlust, refer to outward courage. Inner courage is close to great courage. The courage of humanity and justice is the courage of the noble man, courage that comes from the Way.

The saying that "there is inevitably peril for the bold" refers to outward courage; there is misfortune for the outwardly bold that one must take care to prevent. If you are brave but you are not cognizant of humanity and justice, you will be antisocial, do harm to others, and bring injury on yourself.

Confucius said, "If a noble has courage but no justice, he becomes a rebel. If a commoner has courage but no justice, he becomes a robber." So courage ought to be rooted in justice. Those of unfailing bravery who are humane and just are few.

Confucius also said, "The humane invariably are courageous, but the courageous are not necessarily humane." So it seems that the brave who are humane are few.

Adepts and Masters

An adept, one who is highly skilled, is one who has attained calm. A master, one who has arrived, is one who has attained mastery.

A technician at the stage of mental calm, thoroughly versed in technique and principle, is called an adept. There are also the highly skilled among the aggressive and the clever, but because of their ignorance of technique and principle they cannot be called adepts.

Technicians at the stage where the mind is imperturbable, thoroughly versed in technique and principle, are called masters. So-called experts are masters.

Subtlety

Subtlety is something found in masters. Beyond any rationalization, it cannot be written down or expressed in words.

For example, when Miyamoto Musashi was in warrior training, on his way to Owari he happened to pass by Yagyu Hyogo; Musashi stopped and looked back at him. Hyogo also stopped, and they looked at each other. Musashi said, "I've finally gotten to see a living man! You must be Hyogo, aren't you?" Hyogo said, "Aren't you Musashi?" Then Hyogo brought Musashi home with him. Musashi stayed at Hyogo's house for a long time, merrily drinking wine and playing chess, the two never testing each other's swordsmanship.

This sort of thing is subtlety without rationalization, mind-to-mind communication. Even if you asked Musashi what it meant to "see a living man," Musashi could hardly explain it in words. This sort of thing is called subtlety.

Also, the fact that they never tested their swordsmanship was because they were both masters and each knew the other had no opening, no vulnerability to attack. This can be known without a contest, by behavior and speech.

Resolve

Normally it is fundamental for people to focus exclusively on social norms, but when the time comes it is impossible to gain victory unless you abandon thoughts drawn by lords, parents, wives, and children, forgetting yourself with the attitude that there is no rival facing you and no public behind you.

Of course, the training of resolve must begin with not being afraid of powerful opponents. For example, when you're surrounded by blazing fire, there's no way out; to summon resolve at such a time, you think you can't get out so you might as well die trying to cross the fire. When you leap over that blazing fire, there's one chance in a thousand you'll make it out. If you face a powerful opponent like this, you realize that even if you won't be able to inflict the slightest cut, it would not be an act of courage to stretch out your neck to be beheaded. Even if he is a master, if you determine that you'll at least cut off one of his arms even if you get your head cut off, in the spirit of leaping over a raging fire even if you die in the attempt, you will not easily be defeated no matter how powerful your enemy is.

Once when a servant of a certain master of the One Sword school was summoned by another distinguished personage, toward whom he'd committed a discourtesy, the sword master called his servant to him and said, "You were discourteous to so-and-so, and now he's asked me to turn you over to him. I'm sorry, but I have no choice but to send you to him. No doubt he's going to kill you. Your life is over anyway, so I'll give you my sword and you can go away if you kill me. Otherwise he'll kill you."

The servant said, "What can someone like me, with no skill at all, do to a famous person like you, master? Please excuse me."

The master said, "I've never faced someone who's gone berserk before. It'll serve as a test. So since you're a dead man anyway, I'm taking you on as an opponent for a test. Fight with all your might!"

The servant said, "Well, then, I'll have to take you on." Then when they dueled, the master unexpectedly retreated and was ultimately driven back to a wall. When he saw he was in danger, he shouted and cut his servant down in one fell swoop.

Turning to his disciples, who were watching, he said, "Well, now—going berserk is scary stuff! You shouldn't do things like this for no good reason. If even a menial without skills is like this, how much the more so someone with first-class training—if he were to fight berserk, no one could stand up to him."

The disciples asked, "When you were pressed, were you really pressed, or were you feigning retreat?"

The master said, "I was really pressed. His blade was sharp, and I backed up without planning to."

The disciples also asked, "When you shouted and cut him down, did you kill him because there was an opening?"

The master said, "There was no opening whatsoever, but the kill was subtle."

The subtlety does not come from one's own mind, it is the subtlety of the imperturbable mind.

Even a world-class master was stymied this way by an unskilled menial. Even someone with no skills can do this when he throws his life away.

Anyway, a warrior has to be brave. Reflecting on this, you should train your resolve, beginning with having no fear of opponents; in such a state you'd even leap over a blazing fire. Then a true state of resolve should naturally come about.

This does not, however, mean you should become aggressive. It's a matter of getting rid of timidity and solidifying courage.

If you battle without bravery or any sense of resolve, you'll slash and stab at random in fear of your opponent, losing your presence of mind, confused like someone who's lost his way in the mountains; you won't win once in a hundred battles.

Now, when there's raging fire on all sides and you're in the middle of it, there's no way out. At such a time an ordinary person would weep and wail and lose control and go crazy, and therefore would die before the fire even got to him. So it is with inexpert martial artists when they're going to duel. That's why they can't win.

Real resolve is when, in the midst of fire raging all around, you realize there's no way out, and you sit there calmly, as if you were having a smoke of tobacco, considering it a reminder of the imminence of death; abandoning yourself, you compose your mind and face your adversary forgetful of the opponent before you and forgetful of yourself, just leaving it all up to subtlety. This is absolute resolve.

Kenshin said, "Fate is in heaven, armor is on the chest, accomplishment is in the feet; always fight with your opponent in the palm of your hand, and you won't get wounded. If you fight willing to die, you'll survive; if you fight trying to survive, you'll die. If you think you'll never go home again, you will; if you hope to make it back, you won't. While it is not incorrect to consider the world uncertain, as a warrior one should not think of it as uncertain but as totally certain."

You should reflect on resolve in these terms. Smoking tobacco in the midst of a fire refers to self-abandonment. When perfected, this self-abandonment becomes the imperturbable mind. The imperturbable mind is the secret of warfare.

Demonic Difficulties

There are greater and lesser demons. The greater demons are inner demons, the lesser demons are outer demons. The difficulties caused by greater demons are not demons but are in ourselves. When we're arrogant, we look down on others; when we treat others contemptuously, incidents occur. Are these not great demons that come from ourselves? One who neither fears great opponents nor is contemptuous of lesser opponents is a master.

Lesser demons are devils. Difficulties caused by devils are rare, and even if they exist, as external demons they come from outside, so if you have no vulnerability there's nothing to fear.

Also, even if you are troubled by devils, the trouble is because of your own conceit, so the ego is called the great demon. Since inner demons draw out external devils, all of it comes from one's own conceit.

The interference of the great demon exists within, so it is never apart from one's person. Because the great demon comes from the self, it is not visible yet causes trouble all the time. Realizing this, one should never forget the admonition of sages that troubles caused by the gods may be avoided but troubles you cause yourself cannot be escaped.

Even famous commanders and distinguished heroes of the past may have overcome external demons yet were prone to personal destruction, loss of their domains, and disgrace of their names because of this diabolical king of inner demons. Consider the cases of men like Minamoto Yoshitsune and Nitta Yoshisada. So inferior people like us in these latter days should be a million times more wary against the interference of this great demon.

Two Wheels, Two Wings

Generally speaking, the keys to martial arts are three: practical, theoretical, and psychological.

The practical element is learning the forms and techniques taught by teachers, hardening the body, mastering maneuvers, learning how to strike, stab, parry, and press.

The theoretical element consists of the principles of victory and defeat. These lessons generally teach mastery of calm as a matter of principle. In addition, the forms and techniques that teachers transmit each have a principle. Comprehending them is called theory.

The psychological element is mastery of calm. Mastery of calm is the imperturbable mind.

These elements are likened to a chariot, or a bird in flight. Practice and theory are like the two wheels or two wings, while the mind is like the axle or the body of the bird. If you master practice but don't know principles, you're like a chariot missing a wheel or a bird missing a wing. A chariot cannot run with a wheel missing, a bird cannot fly with a wing missing. If you master practice but don't know principles, even if you win it's not real victory but weakness on the part of your adversary.

Now then, even if you know principles, if you don't practice in action you cannot maneuver freely. It's like a disabled man getting into a fight; he can say what he may, but he can't put up any resistance.

So it is that practice and principle are like two wheels or two wings. When a chariot has two wheels it can run, when a bird has two wings it can fly. But mind is the axle of the chariot, the body of the bird. Without the axle, the chariot cannot move; without its body, a bird cannot fly. Only when the axle is there are the two wheels complete; only with the body are the two wings complete.

Therefore the imperturbable mind is fundamental. When the mind is disturbed, you cannot perform actions or act on principles, because of the way you're affected. To win victory by performing actions and understanding principles is in the imperturbable mind alone. Whoever studies martial arts should cultivate action, principle, and mind to master the secrets of arms.

NINETEEN

HOSHINO TSUNETOMI (fl. ca. 1815)

Hoshino Tsunetomi was learned in classics, history, military science, law, and economics. He was also experienced in government, serving in a number of advisory and administrative positions. Although he was very successful as a prefectural magistrate, looked upon with awe and respect by officials and citizens alike, he made enemies at court by his straightforward and uncompromising manner and was ultimately removed and demoted. Several years later, nonetheless, he was selected to be the personal attaché of the shogun. He fell sick and died while serving in the capital city of Edo. His Shinto-based historical model of the evolution of the samurai caste foreshadowed the official line of the imperial restoration of Meiji in the middle of the nineteenth century.

■ ■ ■

The origins of the samurai may be traced back to when Emperor Jimmu had a sudden rise to power from Miyazaki in the province of Nikko; introducing civilization to primitives, he invaded territory to the east and killed Nagasunehiko. Establishing a capital in Kashiwara in the province of Yamato, he set up an imperial guard. Dividing the imperial militia into two bodies, he had Michiomi-no-Mikoto and Umashimaji-no-Mikoto command them.

The militia commanded by Michiomi-no-Mikoto was called the Kumebe, while the militia commanded by Umashimaji-no-Mikoto was called the Mononobe. The Kumebe waned away over the generations, and only the Mononobe flourished as the shield and citadel of the imperial court. The so-called Eighty Clansmen of the Mononobe mentioned later were these.

The recruitment and the training of the militia up to around the fortieth generation of human emperors are not defined in histories of the nation, but in the forty-fourth generation, during the Yoro era of Emperor Gensei (717–724), Fujiwara no Fuhito (659–720), following an imperial command, devised a legal system based on the six codes of Tang dynasty China. Hence thorough provision was made for the organization of the court, to be the standard for following generations. The work of Mr. Fujiwara must be said to have been great. He was given the honorific title Lord of the Pale Sea; and is it not a result of his contribution that the critical offices of regency have been performed by members of his family generation after generation, even till now?

Although there were minor revisions after that, the overall law was no different. The training and recruitment of soldiers can also be discerned in this connection. After this there were six divisions of imperial guards at court, plus the Hayato and Takiguchi, private bodyguards and swordsmen, no more than two or three thousand.

As for the outer guard, military garrisons were established at Dazaifu and Chinjufu, and a citadel in Akita. When there was to be a punitive expedition, they'd recruit brave and strong men from the farming populations to serve as soldiers, returning them to farming when there was no trouble. A group training officer was permanently stationed in every province to exercise and train farmers in their spare time. People who learned the principle of battle formation and served as soldiers were to that extent even forgiven taxes and corvée.

Ranches were also established here and there in every province, where horses were raised and armed peasants skilled at riding were selected. The ones charged with overseeing these ranches were called the supervisors of the herds, or special managers. In any case, every ranch had to send a certain number of horses to the capital every year as tribute, while the rest were left to the armed peasants to select for use according to their own abilities. So these were not merely expert riders; the legend of 330,000 cavalry throughout Japan comes from this era.

After that, clans such as the Minamoto, Taira, and Fujiwara flourished, and the children and descendants of those who received territory and became provincial governors, prefectural overseers, and so on, continued to reside in these places, while those who stayed in the city but were given manors and estates sent their sons and younger brothers to oversee tax collection. These types gradually produced more and more descendants, and the local people somehow became like their serfs. Having the serfs turn in just a little bit of tax to the provincial government, in spite of sharing what was left over with the serfs, the overseers lacked nothing. So, depending on the size of the territory, as they had also stored armaments, private militias emerged.

The imperial court let this go without thinking ahead, because it seemed convenient for defense to have more soldiers without extra expense. So it was that private militias grew year by year, while recruits for the official army gradually dwindled. With no soldiers going to the group training officers in the provinces, practice and training ceased and the office itself died out, leaving only the private militias of the warrior clans. So they settled on an order among the provinces to take turns every two or three years providing resident guards for the capital, which they called the Royal Watch. The place they were posted was called the place of the warrior, or the place of the samurai.

In this way military clans ran those places generation after generation and had a lot of serfs. Since the state officials were only in office for four-year terms, their power naturally weakened and their administrative orders were not implemented, so they were a government in name only. As long as they got through their four-year stint without incident, they didn't care what happened after that; so even if military clans killed people in private feuds, the state officials would generally pretend not to notice. Even if they had no choice but to notify the capital, requesting a judgment from the bureau of criminal law, the official would only get banished, by the opinion of the jurisprudent. Therefore the military clans took greater and greater liberties, scorning the weakness of state officials.

In those days, security was found in affiliation with a military commander with a reputation, depending on his stature. This fact was the source of the Genpei War (1180–1185), something that didn't happen overnight. [Minamoto] Yoritomo (1147–1199), former lieutenant of the Armed Guard of the Right, raised a volunteer army while in exile, overthrew the Taira clan, and rose to the rank of shogun, in command of all the warriors in the land. Putting protectors in every province and land chiefs on the manors, he brought them all under his control. This was a major change in the system of our country.

Even so, there were still state officials in the provinces sending a certain amount of tax to the imperial court, so the imperial and military orders coexisted. After the rebellion of 1221, however, [when Emperor Go-Toba tried to topple the Kamakura Shogunate], and the war of 1331 [when Emperor Go-Daigo tried to bring down the Kamakura Shogunate], the system of state officers was stopped, leaving only the protectors, so the administration of government wound up distributed among the military clans.

Now then, even among the warriors, only the familiars and

banner men lived near the protectors, while the others all stayed in their own bailiwicks, making their serfs do the farming. Those with few serfs also farmed along with them, and as they became quite friendly with the peasants as a result of this, no matter how badly they might be beaten in a battle with a warlord, it wouldn't reach the point where their base citadel was taken over. Or even if it happened to be taken, in most cases their sons and grandsons wouldn't disperse from the territory but mixed in with the populace, hiding among the peasants, waiting for an opportunity to strike back and retake it.

Distinction between soldiery and farming became extreme with the warlord Toyotomi Hideyoshi (1537–1598). Having acquired the whole land by power, Hideyoshi began the practice of transferring local lords, fearing that if any of the lords in the provinces lived permanently on the land they'd be hard to uproot and eliminate if there was trouble. The fever of the era of the Warring States (ca. 1467–1573) had not yet cooled off. When a domain was changed, because there was no solidarity with the peasants, it was not feasible to distribute military forces, so the samurai were concentrated in castle towns. Even when sufficient time had passed that they could have been settled on the land, because it was profitable and advantageous to keep them living in castle towns, things were left that way. So eventually the time came when samurai were city dwellers. For samurai the leisure and satiety of sitting comfortably eating fine food may seem like great fortune for the moment, but on reflection it might be said that the weakness of warriors and the lack of military preparedness are based on this.

[TWENTY]

HIRAYAMA HEIGEN (1759–1828)

*Hirayama Heigen was a retainer of the Bakufu, the central military govern-
ment under the shogun. His grandfather and father were both famous masters
of swordsmanship, and he grew up with pen and sword in hand. In 1793
he was selected for study at the Bakufu's state college, and in 1796 he was
appointed superintendent of public works. This was not his ambition, so he
resigned on the pretext of infirmity, gave up on an official career, and devoted
himself to study. He studied rites and music, penal law and civil administration, agriculture, sericulture, and waterworks. He was particularly interested in the arts of war, mastering swordsmanship, spear fighting, fistfighting,
archery, shooting, and military science. He wrote several hundred volumes
on military subjects. In 1807 he heard Russia was plundering Ainu territory
and killing Japanese border guards; twice he unsuccessfully petitioned the
shogun to send military forces north against Russia, warning that neglect of
the matter would bring Japan trouble for several hundred years.*

■ ■ ■

Master Xun's discourse on courtesy says, "Those whose view is
life will inevitably die."

This means the same as Wu Tzu's "Those who are eager to
live will die."

On a field of battle, he who becomes absorbed in inevitable
death will survive without trying to stay alive.

Chuang Tzu's chapter on belaboring the mind says, "Respond after sensing, move after being pressed."

Sensing means being affected by feeling; it means the enemy's murderous energy pierces your heart. Response means paying attention. This means that if you pay attention when an enemy's killing energy makes an impact on your mind, then you can stop it before it sprouts. You strike out only when your opponent's sword reaches your body; that way you can take advantage of the ending of the energy. This is also what is meant by the verse

> Lu Shi's sword
> Responds to aggression,
> Acts on sense,
> Adapting endlessly,
> Having no form.

Chuang Tzu's chapter on the sword says, "A swordsman strikes out after the other but hits home before the other."

The idea is to make your body bait to the enemy, slow to begin, so that the enemy cannot restrain himself from lashing out. If you take advantage of that to lash out with your own sword, you receive the end of the enemy's momentum and cut him down with one blow. So even though you wait till after, it's the same as getting there first.

It's hard to express this idea in writing; you have to realize it yourself through personal practice and actual experience. If you understand it wrongly, you'll be calculating whether to strike at seventy versus thirty or at forty versus sixty. How can there be any such thing in a situation where you can be cut asunder in a flash?

In the Nine Songs in the *Elegies of Chu* it says, "Though his head be severed, his heart has no regret."

The word for regret here also means hurt, and it also means to be sorrowful. So it is not only regret. The idea is that even if your head is severed from your body, your spirit is never afraid or injured. If you don't foster the warriors' spirit like this, how can you do your best in the thick of battle?

In "Dragon Strategies," in the section on the momentum of an army, it says, "The successful are decisive, not hesitant; therefore their thunder is so swift you don't have time to cover your ears, their lightning is so fast you don't have time to close your eyes. On the move they're like a stampede, in action they're like mad dogs. Any who try to stand up to them get broken, any who approach them perish."

In the course of combat, if you have such certainty, you won't be hesitating or shilly-shallying, you won't be doubting or wavering, you won't be shrinking back or entertaining reservations, you won't be retreating or giving up. A song on foxes in the night says,

> If a fleet creature looks back at its pursuers,
> They catch it just like that, it is said.
> If a slow creature looks back at its pursuers,
> They stumble and don't catch it;
> So there are many ploys.

It should be understood through the sense of this song that if swordsmen show off affected techniques in swordplay, they all become afflicted with hesitation and doubt. Let the knowing be clean and free.

Wu Tzu's chapter on encouraging soldiers says, "Now suppose a single outlaw ready to die is hiding in the fields, with a thousand men chasing him. All of them are looking around scared—why? Because they're afraid he'll rise up violently and hurt them. This is how one man giving up on life is enough to throw fear into a thousand men."

The sense of this is that if a single outlaw who's expecting to die is hiding out in the plains, why would a huge force of a thousand men in pursuit be looking around scared? Because they're afraid that the outlaw expecting certain death may emerge violently trying to cut them down. So the point is that one man can intimidate a thousand men if he's expecting to die.

Considered from this point of view, in a context of two individuals, if one of them is reconciled to death, he can crush his opponent more easily than breaking dead wood. If one is thinking of successfully killing the other to gain a reputation, while the other moves in relentlessly considering the ground beneath his feet to be his grave, the difference between them is immense.

Wei Liaozi's chapter on organization says, "If one armed man brandishes a sword in a marketplace, everyone will run away from him. It's not that he alone is brave while everyone else is cowardly, but the aims of those certain of death and those intent on life are no match."

In Han Fei's initial interview with the king of Qin he said, "One man who will fight to the death can oppose ten, ten can oppose a hundred, a hundred can oppose a thousand, a thousand can oppose ten thousand, ten thousand can conquer the whole land."

Master Lu's chapter on intimidation says, "When Zhan Shu pledged to die for Lord Tian, the whole state of Qi was scared. When Yu Rang determined to die for Xiangzi, the members of the Zhao clan were all afraid. When Cheng Xing went to his death for the king of Han, the people of Zhou were all intimidated."

These all mean the same thing.

The biography of Kuai Tong in the *Documents of Han* says, "A ferocious tiger that hesitates does not compare to a stinging bee or scorpion. A hero in doubt does not compare to a boy reconciled to death."

It's not that tigers and wolves are not ferocious, and not that heroes are not brave, but if they hesitate and doubt and do not pounce right on their prey, that's equivalent to fear. Then the stinging of bees and scorpions, or the thrust of a boy's dagger, is more fearsome. This is a matter of whether or not you go ahead.

Warriors should realize that when the time comes that they are jousting or dueling in life-or-death situations, those who hesitate and backpedal, or who look back and shilly-shally, all stall here. So the flames of the energy of your will to kill never erupt, your concentration and psychic mass do not penetrate the enemy's heart. You're already in the realm of violence, yet you still hope to keep your fleeting life, cringing in the short shadow of a sword, trying to hide behind the thin shaft of a spear. The base cowardliness of this attitude isn't even worth spitting on. This is getting beaten without making an effort, even leaving disgrace on your corpse. Let the warriors of my band get beyond this demon realm into the domain of the spiritual warrior.

The *Code of the Charioteers* says, "Be decisive and swift with a blade."

Mao Yuanyi said, "When swords cross, you must be resolute and quick."

Once swords cross, if you hesitate, that's the self-centered mind shrinking in fear, timidly retreating. When you break through this self-centered attitude, then sure and swift courage and resolve spring up, like a hungry hawk attacking a bird or a starving tiger seizing an animal. If you attain this, your momentum is unstoppable, like a round boulder rolling down a steep hillside. Sun Tzu, the sage of warfare, also refers to this: "I have heard of military actions that were clumsy but quick, whereas I've never seen any that were skillful yet took a long time." The same text also says, "Once thoughts are settled, your heart is strong, and you advance and withdraw without hesitation."

If you are certain in your resignation to death, then fearful thoughts end, and a brave and strong heart spontaneously arises. With this, both advance and withdrawal are timely and opportune. You are able to enter a subtle state of individual judgment on your own—how could you be burdened by doubts and misgivings?

Advance means advancing on an enemy; withdrawal means returning after killing the enemy. After you've gone forth and killed the enemy, there's nothing to do but withdraw. If you say an enemy is strong and inhibits your advance and withdrawal, then you are not advancing and withdrawing on your own initiative; the meaning is lost.

―――――

Master Lu's chapter on loyalty and integrity says, "According to You Li, a knight only worries about not being brave; why worry about not being skillful?"

What this means is that a warrior should be troubled by lack of courage and firmness in the heart, considering it an illness, and not be disturbed by lack of ambition.

Consider the example of the frontline lancers and the frontline climbers who scale walls. When an enemy army comes rushing at you with the points of their spears in a row, do you imagine you could go forward on the strength of the thought that you'll get a letter of recommendation or a prize for serving as a frontline lancer? The same goes for the men who scale walls; while they're climbing the walls their hands are occupied, so they are exposed to arrows from hidden archers, spears thrust through chinks, or gunfire from snipers. If they climb over a well-defended spot, they are exposed to all sorts of wounds from ambushers with spears and swords stabbing and cutting their legs. Here too, do you suppose they could climb through such violence on the strength of the notion of going home with a feather in their cap? In either case, it is impossible to advance or climb on the front lines unless you step to it with the understanding that this is where you're going to die and now the time to repay your debt to your country has arrived.

Although it is possible to survive ten thousand deaths as a result of this resignation, thus achieving success and elevating your name, nevertheless, as noted at the outset, this is not something you ever count on.

Thus even a skinny man without the strength to carry so much as a bushel of rice, if this brave heart is firm on the field of the warrior's ultimate sacrifice, is this very day a knight capable of facing a thousand men alone. But if his brave heart is not firm, then even a man of great strength and speed, even an incomparable warrior, is nothing to be afraid of.

By the way, this character You Li appears in the *Wu-Yue Spring and Autumn Annals*. He was a very small soldier and had no strength, but though he was such a weak man that he'd be blown over in the wind, yet he slew the prince Qing Ji, a mettlesome fellow even myriad men could not oppose. This can indeed be used as a whetstone to polish the heart of a warrior.

The *Masters of Huainan*, in the lessons on the arts of leadership, says, "No weapon is sharper than mind; even the finest sword is inferior."

What this means is that there is nothing sharper than shattering an enemy's nerve with your mental concentration. Not even a fine sword can compare. This is the doctrine of mental attack, mental warfare. Break the enemy's root, and the branches and leaves will be ruined even if you ignore them. Manual skills are the branches and leaves, the soul is the root—break the enemy's soul, and his skills will become useless.

If you are entranced in a state of pure unadulterated resignation to death, and your will to kill your enemy at any cost pierces straight through the enemy's heart and shakes him up, even highly developed skills will be of no use. At this point, even the sharpest sword isn't worth talking about.

The *Wei Liaozi* says, "A victorious army is like water. Water is extremely soft and yielding, but by erosion it can cause hills to crumble, by nothing but consistent steadiness of pressure."

The sense of this is that an army that prevails over enemies is like water, meaning that everything in its path is destroyed. Water is soft and yielding, but where it causes erosion even hills crumble, because it is the nature of water to form a course and maintain constant contact. Warriors should realize something from this.

Those who practice techniques today, as soon as they face off with an opponent, feint to the right and strike to the left, feint at the hemline and strike at the head. All of them are preoccupied with deceiving and luring, so their murderous spirit never pierces their opponents' chest and gut. As a result, opponents are not fazed at all, so they still perform freely.

What a pity! This way, even if you labor and struggle all your life, it will end up as a scene of living intoxicated and dying dreaming, with no effective fire wall. It is to be hoped that you will be awakened by this principle of water causing hills to crumble if it is concentrated and consistent. Practice the real thing with a true heart and reach the subtle state of independent freedom. If so, then when they are shot by the light of your eyes, enemies cannot face you, almost like people dazzled blind by the morning sun.

The *Masters of Huainan* lessons on military strategy say, "Wind and rain can be shut out, but cold and heat cannot be controlled, because they have no form."

Wind and rain, which have form when they occur, can be blocked out, whereas cold and heat, which occur without form, cannot be shut out or expelled. Now, swords are a man's wind and rain. Opponents have to be able to block and parry to keep them away from their bodies. The spirit is a person's cold and heat; how can it be prevented from piercing the hearts of enemies and shattering their souls? The saying that "nonbeing penetrates even where there is no gap" means the same thing.

The *Masters of Huainan* also says, "When two people cross swords and their skills are no different, it is the brave man who will win. Why? Because of the seriousness with which he acts."

Victory and defeat are not in relative skill; courage or cowardice make the difference. The courageous are unafraid, so they're able to concentrate completely, without distraction. That is how they secure their victories.

People who teach martial arts in the present day are different from this, competing on the basis of skills. Thus you beat someone inferior to you, lose to someone superior to you, and kill someone equal to you at the same time he kills you. This way, even if you labor for years devoting your whole life, what effect will that have? This is just the low-level perception of this type.

At the time of the disturbance of 1449 [when the Oirats invaded China] brave men were recruited from all over the land. A certain man went to the capital, where his skills were tested and found unmatched in eighteen kinds of martial arts, so he was chosen first. Nevertheless, as it turned out he was not distinguished for achievement. Why is that?

From this point of view, victory and defeat cannot be discussed in terms of comparative skill. That is why men famed for skill with sword or spear since ancient times have never been known to achieve anything of merit on a field of combat.

There was a master sharpshooter in Japan who could hit a willow leaf at a hundred paces. He could tell from indoors where birds were gathered on the roof by listening to their cries, so accurately that he could shoot them down without seeing them. That's how skilled he was, yet at the time of the invasion of Korea they say he missed every single shot.

So there's no question of discussing victory and defeat in terms of skill. Nevertheless, if you don't enter in by way of martial arts, you have no method of arousing this state of murderous fury. So practicing martial arts is a matter of course. But if you leave it at the level of theory from books, then in real situations you'll always lose. This is called the literary and verbal art of war.

I am not saying it's wrong for people to practice techniques, I only lament that they don't apprehend the path taught by those techniques. What a pity that there's not a single hero in the land to rise up, demolish decadence, and awaken the deluded from this habit.

The *Liezi*'s chapter on the Yellow Emperor says, "When a drunken man falls from a cart, he may get hurt but doesn't die. His bones and sinews are the same as other people's, but the injury he suffers differs from others' because his spirit is whole."

If a man drunk on wine falls from a cart, he may get injured by the impact, but it won't be fatal, because wine fortifies people's mettle, so the spirit is not fearful but solid. When a warrior stands on a field of contest, if his spirit is whole, his energy is full, and he is clear of thoughts of fear, then arrows and bullets shouldn't hit him.

This is what is meant by the saying from a military text of the Kenshin school that runs, "A straight arrow doesn't work—the shield at the side is pierced through the center." In Lao Tzu's classic it says, "One who is skilled at maintaining life does not run afoul of rhinos and tigers on land, does not wear armor and weaponry in the army. Rhinos have no way to gore him, tigers have no way to claw him, weapons have no way to wound him. Why? Because he has no mortal spot."

An encyclopedia also says that cranes live a long time because there is no morbidity in them. These citations all mean the same thing: a state that is always alert and lively. Gain insight here to master the living potential.

[TWENTY-ONE]

SATO NOBUHIRO (1773–1850)

Sato Nobuhiro was descended from a long line of hereditary physicians. His great-great-grandfather, prompted by a famine, began to study agricultural administration. His great-grandfather, grandfather, and father all continued and developed this line of study, and Nobuhiro consummated this family specialty in the fifth generation, editing his ancestors' writings and also composing his own works. He traveled around studying climate and soil, focusing on boosting production, formulating plans for administrative reform. He also lectured on fishing methods and wrote on ways to preserve fishing villages. He also taught flood prevention and agricultural methods. In one domain where he'd been invited to teach agriculture, he had a "social storehouse" established in every village for famine relief and aid to the destitute. In another domain he had salt fields developed. Elsewhere he convinced a rich merchant to undertake land reclamation, and in another place he promoted the development of horse ranches. In addition, he taught military science to a number of feudal lords, specializing in sea defense and firefighting. He was concerned about the encroachment of the West in the East, and also wrote about Western history. He advocated aggressive national self-defense and was probably the first to concoct a plan for world government based in Japan.

■ ■ ■

There are many overseas who envy the wealth of our Japan and want to annex us. As I reflect on why it is that, in spite of this fact, there have been no foreign invasions for several centuries, I find there are significant reasons. These reasons are as follows.

In ancient times Empress Jingu personally led a military force across the sea, attacked Koguryo, Silla, and Mimana, conquered all of their chieftains, made them dependent states of Japan, and shook China for a time with her awesome repute. For a period of four or five hundred years after that Korea was a dependency of imperial Japan, and every time there was a rebellion a military force was dispatched to quell it, resulting in countless battles with the Three Hans.

Subsequently, in the Koan era of the reign of Emperor Go-Uta (1278–1288), the Mongol Kublai Khan, after having destroyed the Southern Song dynasty and unified China, riding on the momentum of a string of victories, wishing to take Japan, attacked our western seaboard with more than a hundred thousand elite troops, but they were destroyed by the warriors of Kyushu and the whole force was sunk. Only three men got back alive.

After that, residents of Iyo province (in Shikoku), local samurai of Kurushima, Nojima, and Innoshima, gathered their whole clans and formed gangs that sent ships abroad year after year plundering foreign countries, each enriching his own establishment, thus making piracy their business for many years. West from Shandong, Jiangnan, Fujian, Guangdong, and Guangxi in Ming dynasty China, south to the countries of Annam, Guangnan, Champa, Cambodia, Siam, and so on, as well as the islands of Luzon and Borneo—all of them were afflicted by those pirates. These were the feared Wako written of in foreign books.

After that, from 1592 the regent Toyotomi Hideyoshi attacked Korea, chased off the king of the country, and fought the immense army of the great Ming China, defeating them a number of times, causing the world to tremble in awe.

After that, in 1609, the master of the castle at Shimabara burned ships at Aba harbor, burning and drowning four or five hundred Portuguese in the western sea off Nagasaki.

Around this time the lord of the province of Satsuma sent a navy south, invading the south sea islands as he made his way south to attack the country of Ryukyu, depose its king, and make Ryukyu a dependent state of Satsuma.

Until two hundred years ago, myriad nations trembled in fear of Japan's military threat. Basically, the men of those times were all trained in military affairs and extremely bold and fierce in bloody battle, so even the foreigners in Western countries have heard of our reputation, and to this day they still cannot try anything because of that residual threat. Considered from this point of view, I realize Hideyoshi's attack on Korea was an infinitely great achievement for the whole country of Japan. Magnificent!

Even though the barbarians in Western countries cannot try anything because they fear the ferocity that is the heritage of Japan's fierce generals of old, nevertheless they frequently show up, apparently keeping an eye on conditions in our country. An eerie phenomenon indeed. Recently, every year around the tenth day of the third month Western ships always show up off our western seaboard hunting whales for oil. If local fishing vessels approach them, they are very respectful, presenting articles such as glass containers and fine fabrics to make friends with the people. I don't know what country these foreigners are from, but in the summer of 1816 I went to the seacoast to see these foreign ships through a telescope. They are huge black ships decorated with bright red flags, beautiful as flowers. They seemed quite near, perhaps a few miles offshore.

Once two of these black ships came so close the local people got very upset, thinking they might pull into port. They didn't pull into port, however, but went back to deep water offshore where they'd been before. These ships always go away in the last third of the eighth month, they say, no one knows where. Now, because they come regularly every year, the local people have become accustomed to them and no one is suspicious of them anymore. Nonetheless, ships like this should not be ignored.

Between about 1716 and 1741 Russia gradually invaded eastern regions, taking all the territory of Siberia, opening a major port at Kamchatka. From this port they launched a navy, taking the Kuril Islands and reaching our Ainu island of Rasshoro, taking the Aleutian Islands and invading North America as far as northern California. That land is thousands of miles from the homeland capital of Petersburg.

Then there's England, whose military presence has repeatedly become strong enough to cut off parts of many other countries. In recent times they have invaded islands of the South Seas and taken a large country hundreds of miles south of Japan. Moving several tens of thousands of troops there, they named it New England, and set up forts in various places and established governors there to convert and win over the natives. Using this country as a base, they invaded the neighboring islands, gradually expanding their partition and acquisition of territory.

Such is the state of the world in the present age that with so many powerful nations with resources from annexation, if we let down our guard and show any weakness, such that Japan's military threat appears to them to have declined, that reputation will reverberate throughout the entire world at once. Then an increase of invaders coming year after year is absolutely certain.

So, to neglect sea defense is to beckon a major disaster in the wake of ease. Therefore the best plan for safeguarding the country is to drive off foreign ships rigorously every time they come, to demonstrate Japan's military threat more and more, to dishearten and discourage barbarians. Therefore I have worked out a plan for military preparedness to take these bandits.

Here are the preliminaries. Build forts at the harbors and ports of all seaboard provinces and organize and train naval forces. If they are not organized, trained, and thoroughly drilled, they won't be able to perform their function.

The condition of all things between heaven and earth is that those with a superabundance of power utterly overwhelm others, while those with insufficient power are always dominated by others. Therefore the strictest security for the nation is to guard our own country by attacking other countries.

Let me remark that what I'm discussing here is only about protecting our own country. If you want to know how to attack other countries, there's a book I wrote some years ago entitled *Secret Plans for Merger*. But in the present age there isn't anyone who can make good use of even my house maxims—which is why they remain house maxims—let alone *Secret Plans for Merger*. Toyotomi is already dead—alas, it's all over!

Secret Plans for Merger is an argument for total world government based in Japan, so there's a lot in it that has to be kept secret. It's not a book to show to other people. That's why it's called a secret plan.

[TWENTY-TWO]

SAITO TOTSUDO (1797–1865)

*Saito Totsudo was a scholar of classical Confucianism. Born in Edo
(Tokyo), he worked as an educator in the service of a lord. Later he was
appointed a prefect, but soon returned to education. He promoted Western
learning, both civil and military, as well as traditional studies. In 1855 the
shogun Tokugawa Iesada (r. 1853–1858) met with him and tried to hire
him as an official scholar, but he declined, claiming infirmity, and went
back to teaching until he retired in 1859.*

■ ■ ■

The Origin of the Samurai

The duties of samurai are divided into various kinds. There are
positions in administration, there are offices of finance, there
are educators and advisors, there are bodyguards. All of them,
even down to overseers of kitchens and storehouses, are called
samurai and allowed to wear two swords, to provide for security
against the unexpected. Since they are all supposed to take up
their arms and answer the call of duty if there is a rebellion or an
invasion, they are all called warriors.

It may be objected that civil and military offices were separate
in ancient times, and the so-called samurai comes from the time
of the Genpei War, not the ancient system. This is what people say when they don't know the past very well. The division

225

between civil and military bureaus began in the middle ages. It was not in the institutions of earlier eras.

So, in ancient times, when an incident occurred, even though there were nobles and ministers of state, the emperor or empress would personally lead armies to strike down rebels and predators, sometimes even invading foreign states. Since even the emperor and empress thus became commanders of soldiers, obviously there couldn't have been a distinction between the civil and military from the nobles on down. Ever since the middle ages, when the emperors became cloistered and nobles and ministers of state and their subalterns were mostly sons and brothers of people accustomed to fine dining, when they heard the drums of war they would shrink away, cover their ears, and tremble in fear. Since they were useless for anything, clans specializing in arms arose, such as the Minamoto and Taira.

After that the aristocrats got conceited and looked down on military affairs, thinking them the responsibility of soldiers alone, to the point where it is even recorded that no great minister has put on armor since olden times. How mistaken they were in their thinking!

Anyway, the division of civil and military is not seen even in the Sui (589–618) and Tang (618–907) dynasties of China, much less in ancient Chinese military history. In the *Traditions of Mr. Zuo* too it says, "The main tasks of the state are ceremony and warfare," and the emperors and lords also led military expeditions, much as in our own past.

Thus since even emperors and lords became commanders of soldiers, making warfare their job, is it not logical for officers to be called warriors? Indeed, an ancient reading of the ideograph for *officer* is "service." Since there is no greater *service* than military service, whenever the word service is used alone it should be taken to mean military service.

Therefore, among the many tasks of officers, only the officials in charge of warfare and punishment were specifically called officers. This can be seen from the fact that in the *Ancient Documents* it says that Gao Tao [an expert at law who systematized punishments and created prisons], acting as official officer, settled the disturbances that other peoples caused to the Xia, punishing predatory raiders. Even in the Zhou dynasty the superintendent of prisons was called the master of officers, whose subordinate functionaries included local officers and regional officers. Their job was to control violence. This should also prove that *officer* implies "warrior."

In ancient Japanese history, in the time of Emperor Jimmu, Mumashimade-no-Mikoto led the celestial Mononobe warriors to subdue enemies, and he also led domestic warriors, so the profession of the Mononobe warrior guild continued generation after generation by imperial command. This appears in such sources as the *Records of Ancient Matters* and *Records of Japan*.

Now then, while the name of the warriors' guild was Mononobe, it is also read *Mononou* in the *Manyoshu*. The word *mono* means "soldier"; this was used in old expressions for warriors and military equipment, and in later terms for military officers. So the Mononobe were warriors. This is somewhat like the Chinese custom of reading the word *officer* (*shi*) to refer to military service (*shi*). So it's clear that the term *military officer* did not begin with the Minamoto and Taira clans.

Anyway, in China too, up to the time of the Zhou dynasty (1122–255 B.C.E.), since the emperor, nobles, and grandees took military roles, their wealth was such that they'd refer to military preparedness in terms of ten thousand chariots, a thousand chariots, a hundred chariots. Everyone in the country, high and low, noble and common, was included in military preparedness. Thus for each chariot there were three armored knights and seventy-two foot soldiers. The foot soldiers were peasants, while the commanders were gentry. And when aristocrats and grandees were commanders, the aristocrats and grandees served along with the knights. Therefore the sons of aristocrats were knights in that sense even before they took up office. This can be known from the fact that there is a coming-of-age ceremony for knights but not for nobles.

So in ancient times, in Japan and China too, although aristocrats and grandees were not termed warriors, they should all be called warriors. The fact that officers were all warriors is indisputable. In the Country Manners section of the *Classic of Poetry*, the poem "The South of Zhou" says, "On the march, the armed men, the shield and citadel of the lords." It also refers to the right-hand men of the lords.

Now, whereas warriors had been called shield and citadel, or even right-hand men, in the middle ages they were denigrated with the name *attendant* (samurai) and became like servants and slaves of people in long sleeves. They went along with this for a while, but things changed and the warriors turned into overlords, while the aristocrats lost their authority. This was because they lost the original sense of aristocratic knights and looked down on military service.

But the aristocracy is a thing of the past, so there's no point in talking about it. I speak in this vein because I'm afraid warriors in this time of long-standing peace might become like the aristocrats of the past.

Generally speaking, dislike of arms to the point of contempt is due to lack of understanding of their merits. The value and worth of arms can be known by our celestial ancestor's inheritance of a sword, and also by the seven virtues of warriors set forth in the *Zuo Tradition*.

So when the gods and sages governed on earth, they used

both culture and arms, like the two wheels of a chariot or the two wings of a bird. Among conventional Confucians there may be those who irrationally put the punitive operations of Tang and Wu in the context of the courteous abdication of Yao and Shun, so they think arms are secondary. But even before Yao and Shun, the Yellow Emperor had already used arms to settle the land, and only after that did he get to matters of religion, music, and civil administration.

The same is true of Japan. Even though the successive sages Nintoku and Richu governed the land without effort, emperors such as Jimmu, Sujin, and Ojin, who preceded them, did use arms. And it was because of the campaigns of the likes of Futsunushi-no-Mikoto and Takamikazuchi-no-Mikoto that overall peace was subsequently established.

Also, even in the very beginning of civilization, when wild beasts and predatory birds roamed freely, if human beings had had to stand among them, without the advantage of claws and fangs, they would all have been devoured. Therefore divine sages emerged and made weapons to control the birds and beasts, enabling humankind to proliferate.

This was the beginning of arms. People usually think only in terms of tending to go from order to chaos, but from the point of view of the dawn of civilization, the usual progress has been from chaos to order. Were there no effective use of arms, it would be hard to promulgate civic virtues.

This is also the case when we consider the order of the *Book of Changes*. After "Heaven" and "Earth," it only goes through four symbols before it comes to "The Army"—Difficulty, Innocence, Seeking, and Contention. The hardship symbolized by *difficulty* and the immaturity symbolized by *innocence* are the dawn of civilization. Then, if on account of *seeking* for food the conflict of *contention* is caused, an *army* is raised to settle it.

After "The Army" comes "Accord." After "Accord," through "Accumulation of the Small" and "Conduct," there comes "Tranquillity." In the tradition on assorted symbols it says, "'The Army' implies sorrow, 'Accord' happiness." The reason *accord* brings happiness is that *the army* takes the trouble and pain to pacify disruption. Following that, things are accumulated by *accumulation of the small*. After accumulating things, manners of *conduct* develop, bringing the peace of *tranquillity*.

For knights and grandees of the present, having the happiness of accord without the sorrow of *the army*, riding on the peace of *tranquillity*, the easy life living off taxes and exactions is due to the military achievements of their forefathers. If they forget the virtues of arms and get accustomed to arrogant ease, it will produce the disorder symbolized by *tranquillity's* turning to *negativity*. That's why the next symbol after *Tranquillity* is *Negativity*.

Let us be wary of tranquillity's turning into negativity, remember the sorrow and pain of the army, and considering the ultimate danger represented by these symbols in the context of their overall order, never forget warriorhood in a time of general peace, so as to be the nation's claws and fangs and right-hand men.

The Manner of a Warrior

The great men among the knights are the chiefs of the four classes of citizens. Since they serve their lords above and oversee the civilians below, their manner has to be correct. For a knight, correct manner is centered on courtesy and justice, honesty and integrity. In recent times the manner of knights has deteriorated daily, first getting carried away by arrogance, eventually to fall into weakness, almost to the point of losing all sense of courtesy, justice, honesty, and integrity.

To correct this degeneracy, first we must value a simple and stolid manner. Then we can become courteous, just, honest, and conscientious too. Simple stolidity is the basic character of the warrior; since being the claws and fangs of the state lies in this, we should always be this way.

Now then, manner refers to normal habit, so those in the warrior class, even three-year-old children, should learn to be ashamed of weakness and take pleasure in strength, being shamed and rebuked as cowards if they get scared or startled.

Although people are more or less strong or weak by nature, warriors should aim only for strength, avoiding weakness, enduring even things that are frightening and disturbing, not evincing anything in words or appearance—then they are reliable. If you ordinarily get startled or frightened by inconsequential things, you won't be able to wield spear and sword in a hail of arrows and bullets to drive off enemies. At times like that, the foremost duty of a knight, the foremost honor, should be to die in front of his lord's horse, never retreating a single step. So you should always maintain this manner and cultivate courage, not being startled by thunder, unhesitating in conflict, not letting your expression change even if a mountain should crumble right in front of you.

Since ancient times, anyone known as a warrior has been like this, but as general peace has continued for a long time, this manner has weakened somewhere along the line, and the sons of knights even do their best to avoid cold, heat, and hard work. Some are even afraid of snakes or scared of thunder, like women and girls. They are even worse than the soldiers of the western provinces ridiculed by Saito Sanemori for complaining about the summer heat and winter cold when out on campaigns.

Knights are also human beings, so they are similarly affected by the miseries of cold and heat, sickness and pain, but because they fear to degrade their honor and disgrace their office, they forbear. Some people, though, seeing them controlling themselves this way, deride it as pride. What are they thinking? How strange! The ways of knights are of great importance, connected with the prosperity or decline of the nation; so everyone should be influenced by an air of strength, so that even a physical weakling would have a heart outstanding among myriad men.

The Song dynasty Confucians teach transformation of the temperament, so by keeping this attitude, even the weak will become strong. For now, observe the maxim "Self-mastery comes from continuing to overcome those biases of nature that are difficult to conquer," while over the long run practicing the adage "When down and out, prevail by firmness." If you don't forget, day or night, eventually you'll develop an air of strength and fortitude.

In recent times, Emperor Go-Komei (r. 1846–1867) was afraid of thunder, so he studied Cheng-Zhu [neo-Confucianism] and worked on transformation of temperament, eventually losing his fear. This is excellent.

Anyway, to conduct yourself in a strong manner, first you must maintain a manner of simplicity and austerity. The softening and weakening of knights is due to a tendency toward luxury and extravagance. If you adopt a manner of simplicity and austerity, that in itself will be close to a manner of strength and fortitude.

That is why farmers, who work in the fields, being simple in their ways, are mentally firmer than merchants and physically more robust. Therefore the manner of a warrior may well be close to that of a farmer but should by no means be anything like that of a merchant. Even if his salary is small and he is poor, and he has no choice but to do something to augment his income, a samurai still wouldn't do anything like a merchant. There should be no objections, however, to doing work such as fishing, hunting, farming, gardening, rice pounding, and woodcutting.

One of the Mikawa knights, a man of the Kondo clan, used to hire himself out to farmers as a laborer because his family was poor. Once when he was working in the fields, Tokugawa Ieyasu passed by exercising his falcons. With no way to conceal himself, Kondo knelt down, muddy as he was, in extreme deference. Seeing this, the shogun admired his will and didn't blame him; indeed, he even increased his salary. So it should be acknowledged that the manner of a warrior may acceptably be close to that of a farmer.

In the *Records of Manners* too, a son of a knight who has come of age is referred to as able to carry kindling, while one still young is referred to in terms of being as yet unable to carry kindling. Also, when a knight is ailing, it is a courtesy to refer to his condition as an affliction from gathering firewood. We can see how the manner of knights of ancient times aimed at simplicity.

If knights personally do menial labor, not only will they be physically robust but they will also remain frugal and simple, so the way of life in their houses becomes richer, as a result of which they can have plenty of weaponry on hand too.

As warriors, it goes without saying that knights should have weaponry at hand. But it is also desirable to have plenty of men and horses at the ready as well. No matter how brave at arms you may be, you can hardly achieve anything by yourself alone. Since olden times, most men of outstanding reputation have depended on good horses and good cohorts to achieve their success. So it is desirable to have men and horses on call, even if beyond your means.

In the past, both upper and lower ranks concentrated on military preparedness. So as long as one was to be a knight, even with a salary of only fifty *koku*, generally one would have a horse, they say. In China too, in the time of the Zhou dynasty they valued culture, but they still attended to military preparedness as well. In the *Records of Manners* it says the wealth of grandees was expressed in terms of horses and chariots. They were all referred to in terms of military equipment, as grandees having a hundred chariots, feudal lords having a thousand chariots, and the emperor having ten thousand chariots, much as we refer to them today by the amount of rice they receive, such as so many thousand or so many tens of thousands of *koku*. Concern for military preparedness is evident.

In the past, knights minimized their expenditures on clothing and food, taking an interest solely in military preparedness, so they were all frugal. Once upon a time a chief officer of eastern Japan, although he was head of the warriors of eight provinces, didn't even have a change of clothes. It is related that once when a guest came he said, "I'm just doing my laundry, so I'm naked; please wait a while." Though this is being excessively frugal, it shows how people of the past had no craving for clothing and food but focused on military preparedness.

Samurai now, even men with large salaries, strain their finances with luxury. Not only are they lax about military equipment, they hardly get any exercise, and on top of that they overindulge in food and drink. So lots of them are sickly. Men without some sort of ailment like dyspepsia or lumbago are so rare that at gatherings of samurai it has become customary to talk about who has what illness, the way you might talk about the weather. The development of such a habit is extremely unpleasant, since the predilection of warriors is to be ashamed of weakness and grit their teeth and bear pain and discomfort in silence.

A saying of Confucius goes, "Spending all day in company without the conversation touching upon duty, indulging in exercise of petty wit—I have trouble with this!" When knights meet friends, if they speak of their aspirations, refine their loyalty and their respect for parents, and reflect on the warrior's way, this could be called conversation touching on duty. So to spend the days bragging about luxuries should be called shameless and immoral.

So it is only when you become strong and sturdy in your ways that you can attain a sense of courtesy, justice, honesty, and integrity. If a knight's sense of courtesy, justice, honesty, and integrity weakens, what will become of him in the end? It's worrisome. In *Guanzi* it says, "Courtesy, justice, honesty, and integrity are the four mainstays of a nation. If these four mainstays are not tight, the nation collapses." Ah, can we be unconcerned?

The Warrior Spirit

Once the manner of a knight is proper, it is essential to cultivate the warrior spirit. While maintaining the manner of a knight is for the purpose of cultivating the warrior spirit, insofar as manner is a matter of external appearance, however awesome it may be, it cannot be relied upon on a deep level. When the spirit fills your being like blazing fire, that is rather more reliable.

Thus, it is when the warrior spirit is effective that the manner of the knight is truly firm. Even if your physical strength is above ordinary, if your spirit flinches you can't face opponents effectively. However skillful you may be in martial arts, if your spirit flinches you can't use them against opponents. So, it is when filled with spirit that intelligence and courage are effective.

For this reason a horse is not prized for its color but for its sturdiness; in a warrior it is not sternness of appearance that is valued but strength of spirit that is approved.

It is this spirit that plunges into the thick of battle. What speaks directly and criticizes severely right in the ruler's face is also this spirit. When your dignified manner in everyday life is so dashing that people are in awe of you, that too is due to being filled with this spirit.

If you are not filled with spirit, you become gutless. Once you're gutless, you'll be spineless too. What use is a spineless warrior?

In recent times the manner of knights has deteriorated greatly, some being as soft as women, some being as mean as merchants. How can men like this perform the role of shield and citadel? They might as well break their bows and arrows and swords and give up the samurai profession. Even those among them who are said to be warrior-like may seem impressive when suited up and wearing their swords, but most of them while outwardly stern are inwardly soft. They may contemptuously rebuke weak people like widows and widowers, but when they encounter strong people they remain silent where they should criticize. How could such timid samurai be right-hand men of nobles and lords?

These bad habits all come from pampering oneself and being greedy. Confucius said of a certain man, "He is greedy—how can he be firm?" So if you want to be firm and unflinching in spirit, first you should control desire, as it says in the *Book of Changes*. It is only out of greedy desire that you think you might as well flatter your superiors for the sake of a profitable salary, or you think you might as well bow your head to merchants for the sake of money.

Mencius said, "Shame is a serious matter for a man." A samurai without a sense of shame shouldn't be called a knight. Knights of old "could be killed but not disgraced," considering it a serious detraction for a knight to be shamed, determined not to be dishonored even if they're killed. So even if they were executed for a crime, they considered it an honor to be allowed to cut their own guts. They disdained being tied up, as a disgrace to the corpse.

Generally speaking, the sorts of men who are to be punished are not good people, so there should be no question of honor or disgrace. The reason such men were nonetheless so brave is that in the past no warrior, whether good or bad, was shameless and clueless in the way of the warrior.

The fact is that it is by having warriors that a nation stands, and it is by having spirit that a warrior stands. If a warrior's spirit is not strong, that's like ginger that's not spicy. What flavor is there? With only knights like this, it's the same as having no knights—how can the nation stand?

Anyway, that spirit comes from having a sense of shame and forgetting desire. This is what is called the heart of honesty and integrity. When you forget desire, you don't shirk your duty even if it's bad for you personally, and if you have a sense of shame, you won't be fazed by anything, even the prospect of being killed. This way you won't be afraid of anything in the world. Isn't this strength?

Mencius said, "A man of will doesn't forget he may wind up in a ditch, a brave man doesn't forget he may lose his head." If samurai always keep this maxim in mind as a protective amulet, they will not lose the sense of honesty and integrity. Not losing the sense of honesty and integrity, they will also become courteous and just.

The Discipline of the Warrior

Once you're filled with the warrior spirit, it is best to keep the discipline of a warrior. The word for discipline originally comes from the word for the joint in bamboo. Bamboo has the energy to grow to the sky, but were it not for regular joints, it could not weather snow and frost and survive the four seasons without changing color. Likewise, if the conduct of a warrior is only spirited and not disciplined, how can he really be effective?

Therefore in everyday life a warrior observes the discipline of taking nothing from anyone, while if he encounters trouble he keeps the discipline of a loyal subject who does not serve two rulers; on the border of life and death, he follows the doctrine of being faithful to principles even unto death and not being discouraged when facing an immense task. Only then is it really useful to be spirited. This is the sense of courtesy and justice. Otherwise, even if you have the temperament to think lightly of death, it is not merely ineffective but actually harmful.

Chuang Tzu said, though, "Death and life are both important." Death is something people fear, not an easy thing, so you need to have an understanding of it in everyday life. While any samurai who is someone's son generally understands that his life belongs to his lord, since ancient times not a few have lost their discipline to save their own worthless lives. Some may temporarily get excited about dying for a righteous cause, but those who can hold out firmly to the death through countless upsets and reversals in the midst of trouble have been very rare, even in the past.

Therefore, even though the house of Tokugawa had many loyal retainers and dutiful knights, when Tokugawa Ieyasu was preparing a residual defense for Okazaki at the time of the battle of Maki (versus Hideyoshi, 1584), he put Honda Shigetsugu in charge because he figured that if worse came to worse he'd be the only one to kill his own wife and children and die unflinching with the castle as his pillow. Even in the old days it was considered hard to find men who were constant in discipline like this, dying unfazed.

Even so, the Tokugawa establishment had a lot of disciplined and dutiful warriors. When Tokugawa Ieyasu and Toyotomi Hideyoshi declared a truce, at their first meeting Hideyoshi asked Ieyasu about the treasures of the house of Tokugawa. Ieyasu replied that he had nothing, but when pressed for an answer he then responded, "I have five hundred men who will plunge into water and fire for me, caring less for their lives than dew or dust. This is my treasure." Considering this, with so many men steadfast to the death, it is no wonder the Tokugawa took over the land.

Before that, there had never been so many warriors faithful to the death as at the time of the destruction of the Hojo. When Hojo Takatoki committed suicide in Kamakura, several thousand men killed themselves along with him. Several hundred men also cut their guts along with Hojo Nakatoki. Besides them, untold numbers in the provinces died. We can infer the strength of the warrior spirit in those days. Even so, while the Hojo did wrong, no one criticized their wrongs or stopped their infidelities; they drew their bows and brandished their swords against the orthodox emperor, so they can hardly be considered models for knights.

In our own sovereign nation of Great Yamato, over a period of more than two thousand years, the only man who can be considered a model for knights is Lieutenant General Kusunoki. The honorable Kusunoki raised a volunteer army at the request of the orthodox emperor. His whole family, even the servants, stayed faithful to the cause, with sons replacing fathers who died, younger brothers taking up after elder brothers who died. Even after several generations they kept the lieutenant general's instructions and protected the imperial house to the death. In this Kusunoki came out far better than the likes of China's Zhang Xun or Tian Wenxiang. In terms of winning people's hearts by his virtue, he stood even better than Zhuge Kongming.

So even among those who die being loyal and dutiful there are such great differences in depth that to be a warrior requires constant polish. Indeed, loyalty and respect for parents are the main measures of human ethics, so if you don't fulfill both you shouldn't be called human. Therefore people lacking in loyalty and respect for parents are worthless no matter how good they may be in other respects. As Luan Cheng said, since your debts of gratitude to your ruler, father, and teacher are second to none, in emergencies you should only go to your death where they are.

So ruler and father, like the sky, are inescapable; in an emergency, there is no choice but to repay them with death. When Confucius said, "In serving your father, make your best efforts; in serving your ruler, devote your very life," he was just using parallelism to show what's essential; in reality, in serving your father you should not only make your best efforts but also devote your very life, and in serving your ruler too you should not only devote your very life but also make your best efforts. This is the same as the statement of Li Taibo of Song, that as a son one dies for respect for parents, while as a subject one dies for loyalty.

Generally, in serving rulers and fathers there are various rules to understand for normal times as well as emergencies. It is essential to always be studying them to keep them in mind, find their appropriate application, and take care to carry them out faithfully and genuinely.

The Heart of the Knight

Once spirited and disciplined, one may be called a good knight. However, since the heart is the source from which spirit and discipline emerge, it is by cleaning the source that the flow will be clear.

Every part of the body has its desire; if the heart is not upright, it will be hard for spirit and discipline to stand. So though the heart is in the chest, as it is the ruler of the whole body, it might be better to say there is nothing apart from it.

First, as to how a knight's heart should be, it is best to aim for the Way. That is why there is the saying in the discourses of Confucius, "A knight aspires to the Way." Since the ideograph for *aspiration* is composed of the ideographs for *knight* and *heart*, the heart of a knight must have an aspiration. And when it comes to aspiration, there is nothing worth aspiring to but the Way. If you aspire to the Way, you should wish to become wiser and wiser, governing yourself and governing others.

Asked what a noble man is, Confucius replied, "Cultivate yourself by being respectful, cultivate yourself to give others security." This is governing yourself and governing others. Master Cheng of the Song dynasty said, "Knights seek savants, savants seek sages, sages seek celestials." This is the will to become wiser and wiser.

To maintain a knight's will to govern self and govern others, there is a constant heart, and there is mental labor. As for a constant heart, Mencius said, "Those who have a constant heart even without a constant livelihood are only the knights." This is the heart that remains unshaken even on the border of death and life, even in the midst of poverty, misery, and hardship. As for mental labor, Mencius said, "Some labor mentally, some labor physically. Those who labor physically feed others, those who labor mentally are fed by others. Those who are fed by others govern others, those who feed others are governed by others." This implies the attitude of compassion and concern for the people.

So a constant heart is the fidelity of knights, mental labor is the economy of knights. It might be objected that the economy is to be run by those who govern the people and the land, so it's questionable whether one should act without the appropriate office, but that is not so—in general, knights are at the top of the four castes; as they eat without tilling and wear clothes without weaving, how could they not have some means of repaying the labor of those who do the tilling and weaving?

Even so, Mencius says, "When in straits, just conduct yourself well; when successful, do good for the world too." So as knights also have their ups and downs, there must also be differences in their behavior according to the time. Confucius warned against strategizing for government if you are not in such a position, so it is not good to assert yourself. Yet a means of doing good for the world has to be understood ahead of time, or else it won't be possible to put it into effect all at once, so you should reflect on the past, study the Way, and master both culture and arms. This is a means of doing good for the world that should not differ in straits or success.

Lu Donglai's maxim for officials says, "Mental labor does not compare to physical labor," cautioning us that a knight's mental labor in doing his best at his job is not as good as the farmers' constant labor feeding people. Isn't it embarrassing?

Once I was on an outing with two or three knights late in the autumn when the farmers were busy taking in the rice harvest. I said to my companions, "All of us live easily on salaries of one or two hundred *koku*. Isn't a stroll such as this due to the benevolence of the ruler above and the work of the farmers below? It takes ten or twenty families working day and night like that, wives and children included, just to support one of our families. So if we spend our days idly, neglecting our professional roles, we'll suffer divine punishment."

So this means a knight should labor with his mind. More-over, though it isn't good to be forward, Master Cheng said that people ranked as knights and above should have an attitude of love for people. A knight is only a real knight when he has this sympathetic heart.

This means governing self is heart, governing others is heart, loving people is heart; everything else has to do with heart too, so you have to study the heart. Study of the heart may seem like Zen study, but Zen is a path studied by people who wither in mountain forests; even if they have settled their minds they are far from the principles of social norms, so that is quite different from what I'm talking about here.

But latter-day scholars sometimes take ritual, music, and literature for scholarship, or they consider extensive reading and strong memory to be scholarship, or they take glossing and annotating to be scholarship. Though these are all partial aspects of scholarship, if you take them alone to be learning, you'll acquire the bad habit of obsession with externals, which will hardly fulfill the basic purpose of governing yourself and governing others.

Were I to speak to scholars such as these, I'd say that scholarship means studying the heart and mind. It's fundamentally different from Zen study and also different from doctrines such as those of Lu Xiangshan and Wang Yangming.

In recent times there's something called Mind Studies, which may be called an accessible doctrine for ignorant men and women. It is not good for knights and great men because it is too soft.

The study of heart and mind I'm talking about can be inferred from the context of this discourse. In any case, if it's not good from the heart, nothing can be good. Where could the teaching of Mencius come from if not the heart? Therefore Mencius said, "The path of learning is nothing but seeking the free heart." There can be no real learning apart from making the heart upright and the mind sincere. But if you just look for the heart and mind without any purpose, that will become Zen study, or an aberrant technique. So you should not seek your subjective mind but rather seek the heart of the Way.

The Way of the Knight

For a knight to govern himself and govern others, first he must govern his heart and mind, but it is not good to do it with the subjective mind; it must be found in the heart of the Way.

The heart of the Way is in everyone's mind; that is to say, it is nature. Although no one is bad by nature and everyone is good, a lot of people are blinded by selfishness associated with human desires. Though there are some good ones among them who aren't blind, as they understand one side they are ignorant of another. None but sages are as clear as the cloudless sky.

So sages are the only ones in whom the heart of the Way is completely clear, and their actions and statements have become the Way, the doctrines that people should keep generation after generation. Even as the Way of sages, though, it's not that it isn't in everyone's heart; it's just that there's a difference between partiality and totality. Seen from the biased point of view of the subjective mind, there are doctrines that sometimes seem stupid; genuine scholarship would be to consider this impression your own shortcoming, have deep faith in the sages, and investigate and clarify their Way, applying it to present-day human relations, seeking the most appropriate of principles.

The true path of the knight is only to be practiced in accordance with this Way, but military clans in recent times have their own so-called bushido. I don't know who defined it, but while some is in accord with the Way, there is a lot that does not escape subjective bias. Just to mention one or two points, there are those who consider it loyalty to cut their guts after their lords die, or consider it justice to take in defectors. These are what Mencius calls unjust morals. The worst are those who have even come to call slash-and-grab robbery a practice of warriors. Though strength is considered essential for warriors, unless it is based on the Way of sages it can degenerate into predation.

Even if you are spirited and disciplined and you slight death, you may still act in ways that violate gallantry and justice, so the true path of the knight is to understand the Way of sages and seek the most appropriate principles.

When Tokugawa Ieyasu began to govern the land, he was dismayed by the fact that people's hearts had been so violent since the Muromachi rule, with many cases of subjects killing lords and sons killing fathers. In order that people might know the Way, he recruited Confucians, promoted learning, and had lots of classics and histories printed and circulated. Many distinguished scholars emerged, not only from his own clan and major retainers, but also from among the people of the other feudal chieftains, ultimately to produce the present state of complete order. It is as different from an uncivilized era like the Muromachi as day is from night. Never having degenerated into chaos again once order was established, this regime is as remote from the Muromachi's constant chaos and demise in disarray as the sky is from the earth. The excellence of civilized qualities is evident.

Anyway, even in the Muromachi era, men of merit who were considered good, such as Hosokawa Yoriyuki and Imagawa Sadayo, were not uneducated. Nevertheless, I don't even like to talk about the men who served the Muromachi regime, so I'll leave them aside for now. Before them, serving the orthodox emperor with complete loyalty and great fidelity outstanding in history, it is men like Lieutenant General Kusunoki and Miyake

Takanori who can be said to have been competent in both culture and arms.

While Miyake Takanori was born into the military, he chose to read books. When Kusunoki was dying, in his last instructions to his son Masayuki he included an admonition to study more and more. So, while loyalty and righteousness were natural in such men as Kusunoki the elder, Kusunoki the junior, and Miyake Takanori among the warriors, and such aristocrats as Fujiwara no Fujifusa and Kitabatake Chikafusa, the reason they were clear about their cause and had no regrets was their learning. Though there were some heroes after them who had cultural ability, beginning with Shingen and Kenshin, the only ones with real learning were Maeda Toshiie and Kato Kiyomasa. The times being what they were, they didn't study widely, but they put what they learned into practice far better than today's scholars.

In scholarship knights should follow the legacy of Tokugawa Ieyasu near at hand, while aspiring from afar to real learning like that of the emperor Nintoku and the prince Uji no Wakiiratsuko. In the middle ages, Emperor Tenchi and great ministers such as Nakatomi no Kamatari and Sugawara Michizane had some success through real learning, but the rest, emperors and ministers alike, admired the splendor of Sui and Tang China, imitating Chinese styles even in attire and administrative organization. Their ritual, music, and cultural artifacts were beautiful, but it was just empty embellishment, and there does not appear to have been any who practiced the true Way of sages. This is worthless, like buying a treasure chest but returning the jewels. If they were really going to study the Way of sages, the classics should have been enough—they wouldn't have gone so far as to send envoys to China. Idly imitating the decadent ways of a foreign country in a late stage of its history and losing the pristine simplicity of their own nation, they also made a religion of Buddhism, which is humane and gentle, distorting the regal law, so they became effete, and this resulted in the deterioration of the imperial house.

Scholarship is basically not a matter of studying Tang dynasty Chinese culture but studying the Way of China; it is not studying a Chinese way, for the Way of the sages of China cannot be different from the ancestral Way of our own sovereign nation. Although the virtues of our ancestral deities were superior to the sages of China, because there was no writing in those times, no detailed account has come down. When the Way of sages happened to be transmitted to his court, the sage emperor Ojin heartily approved of it, and that is why he had his princes study it too.

Well, then, when Prince Osasagi became emperor, he ignored the dilapidated condition of the imperial palace and forgave several years' taxes to enable the populace to prosper, not disgracing his posthumous name Nintoku, which means "humane." When Prince Uji deferred the throne to his older brother and the older brother refused, Uji ended his own life to make his brother emperor. In this he was superior even to Taibo and Bo Yi.

It was because they ably followed the Way of sages in their character and their administration that theirs could be called true learning. In the middle ages there may have been an appearance of culture, but it was empty embellishment, not real culture.

GLOSSARY

Akechi Mitsuhide (1526–1582) A warrior in the organization of the powerful Japanese warlord Oda Nobunaga. He ultimately turned against Oda and killed him.

Akita A province in the northwest of Japan's main island (Honshu).

Ancient Documents The *Shang Shu*, a Chinese classic purporting to contain seminal documents from ancient dynasties.

Annals of Mr. Lu By Lu Buwei (Lu Donglai; ca. 291–235 B.C.E., q.v.), chancellor of the state of Qin from 251 to 246 B.C.E. Lu was an advisor to the First Emperor of China.

Ashikaga Shogun, Third Ashikaga Yoshimitsu (1358–1408, r. 1368–1394); united the northern and southern imperial courts of Japan in 1392, ending more than fifty years of division and conflict between competing factions in the imperial system, which coexisted with the Bakufu, the military government under the Shoguns.

Ashikaga Takauji (1305–1358) The founder and first shogun of the Ashikaga Shogunate of Japan, founded in 1338, inaugurating the Muromachi era, most famous for its weakness and corruption.

Awa and Sagami Provinces of old Japan, on the east coast, on opposite sides of a major inlet, thus considered critical points of naval defense.

249

Berserking An ancient practice found among various peoples, including Rajputs, Celts, and Vikings, consisting of creating a temporary psychosis for the purposes of combat. The Japanese term used here for such a state, *shinimonogurui,* literally means "the frenzy of a dying creature."

Book of Changes The *I Ching,* one of the Chinese classics. Popularly considered a divination text, it was used by Confucian scholars to describe situations, trends, and events in terms of relations and changes.

Book of the Shadow of the White Flag A work by Li Quan of Tang dynasty China, a military scientist and Taoist devotee. Steeped in the strategic work attributed to the Yellow Emperor (q.v.), he wrote a well-known commentary on Sun Wu's military classic *The Art of War,* translated in Thomas Cleary, *The Art of War,* 1988.

Bo Yi (twelfth century B.C.E.**)** A noble of the Shang dynasty of ancient China who retired into the mountains and starved to death after the demise of the dynasty, refusing to pledge fealty to the Zhou dynasty, which supplanted the Shang. Although the Zhou is usually considered superior to the Shang in normative Zhou literature, Bo Yi is a Confucian hero and an icon of the virtue of loyalty.

Cao Cao (155–220) One of the principal warlords of China's Three Kingdoms era, immortalized in literature. For Cao Cao's commentary on The *Art of War* by Sun Wu, see Thomas Cleary, The *Art of War,* 1988.

Cheng, Master This name can refer to either of the two famous Cheng brothers who were influential neo-Confucians of Song-dynasty China, Cheng Hao (1032–1085) or Cheng Yi (1033–1107). The Cheng brothers were among the founders of neo-Confucian idealism. For Cheng Yi's commentary on the *I Ching,* see Thomas Cleary, *The Tao of Organization: The* I Ching *for Group Dynamics,* 1995.

Cheng Bushi A Chinese general and borderland governor who fought along with Li Guang (q.v.) against the Huns in the second century B.C.E.

Chengsang tribe An ancient people, neighbors of the ancestors of the Chinese, mentioned in Wu Qi's *Art of War*, who are said to have abandoned military preparedness and lost their territory as a result.

Chinjufu A center of regional military administration on the eastern seaboard of Japan, in the province of Mutsu, probably established during the Nara period (710–794). In 1871 it was made into a naval headquarters.

Chuang Tzu (Zhuangzi) A famous Chinese writer of the fourth century B.C.E., whose book is conventionally considered a classic of Taoism.

Classic of Poetry The *Shi Jing*, a collection of ancient Chinese poetry and song, a primary classic of Confucianism.

Code of the Charioteers A classic Chinese military text. For excerpts see Thomas Cleary, *Ways of Warriors, Codes of Kings*, 1999.

Cut the gut Seppuku, vulgarly known as hara-kiri, the favored method of suicide for samurai. In executions or individual suicides an assistant (*kaishakunin*) would finish by beheading, but it is not clear whether the mass suicides of the fourteenth century were concluded in this manner, considering the circumstances and conditions.

Dazaifu The Japanese imperial office governing Kyushu during the Heian era, from the eighth to the twelfth centuries, which served as a reception center for embassies from China and Korea.

Di Renjie (seventh century) Held numerous important offices in Tang dynasty China. He was repeatedly dismissed and relieved of duties for political reasons but was also credited with many successes.

Divine Warrior A name for the Shinto war god, and for the first emperor of Japan, according to Shinto legend.

"Dragon Strategies" Part of the *Six Strategies*, a famous Chinese classic of military science attributed to Lu Shang, mentor of the founder of the Zhou dynasty in the twelfth century B.C.E. For selections from the *Six Strategies*, see Thomas Cleary, *Ways of Warriors, Codes of Kings*, 1999.

Eighteen realms A Buddhist term for the totality of ordinary experience, consisting of six sense faculties, six sense consciousnesses, and six domains of sense data.

Elegies of Chu A very famous Chinese literary monument, a collection of poetry by Chu Yuan (340–278 B.C.E.) of the southern state of Chu, which was anciently associated with early Taoism.

First Emperor of China (260–210 B.C.E.) Founder of the Chinese empire. King of the state of Qin from 247 to 241 B.C.E.; united the ancient states of China under Qin rule by 221 B.C.E.

First ruler of Shu After the collapse of the Chinese Han dynasty in 220, a continuation was briefly established from 221 to 265 in the region of Shu, modern-day Sichuan. The first ruler reigned from 221 to 223.

Five Things Five bases of comparison, according to Sun Wu's *The Art of War*, by which the relative strength of military forces may be assessed: morale, weather, terrain, leadership, and discipline.

Four dispositions A Buddhist term for types of human delusion and bondage, characterized as demonic, ghostly, animalistic, and titanic. These stand for manifestations of greed, aggression, and folly.

Fujiwara no Fujifusa (1296–1380) A member of the powerful Fujiwara clan who served Emperor Go-Daigo in the latter's struggle for imperial restoration in medieval Japan; attempted to wrest national power back from the Shoguns.

Futsunushi-no-Mikoto A Shinto deity, an apotheosized figure of prehistoric times represented as negotiating the cession of Izumo province to Yamato. Futsunushi-no-Mikoto is especially associated with martial arts; he is honored at the Katori Shrine in Chiba prefecture. The oldest school of martial arts in Japan, the Tenshin Shoden Katori Shinto Ryu, founded in the fifteenth century, is associated with this shrine and this deity.

Gao Tao An archetypal figure from the *Ancient Documents*, minister of the ancient Chinese ruler Shun (third millennium B.C.E.), represented as an expert on law who systematized the penal system and created prisons.

Genpei War (1180–1185) A protracted conflict between two leading samurai clans of Japan, the Taira and the Minamoto. This war ostensibly broke out over the issue of choice of emperor, with each of the two great clans supporting a different candidate. The Minamoto defeat of the Taira turned out to be a prelude to the establishment of the first central military government, the Bakufu, under the authority of shogun Minamoto Yoritomo.

Go-Daigo, Emperor (1288–1339) A particularly famous emperor in Japanese history, Go-Daigo plotted to overthrow the military government in Kamakura. He also opposed the rising warlord

Ashikaga Takauji, who was to found the second military dynasty in Muromachi.

Go-Komei, Emperor (r. 1846–1867) The predecessor of the illustrious Meiji emperor of Japan, the central figurehead of the Meiji Restoration propelling Japan into modern industrialism, international commerce and warfare, and colonialism and imperialism.

Go-Toba, Emperor (1180–1239) Enthroned in childhood as emperor of Japan, Go-Toba was forced to abdicate in 1198 by Minamoto Yoritomo, the shogun who founded the first Bakufu, or supreme military government, in Kamakura. Go-Toba reigned as a cloistered emperor (that is, from behind the veil of a Buddhist order) from 1198 to 1221. In 1221 he staged a rebellion to overthrow the Bakufu and restore imperial rule, but he was defeated in the attempt.

Great Goddess Lighting the Sky Same as the Great Goddess of Ise: Amaterasu Omikami, the goddess of the sun, tutelary deity of the imperial clan of Yamato, later Japan, center of the imperial Shinto cult.

Great Goddess of Ise The Shinto sun goddess, tutelary deity of the Yamato imperial clan.

Guan Zhong (725–645 B.C.E.) Guan Yiwu, an erstwhile soldier, merchant, and political scientist of the Spring and Autumn era of China. He is the nominal author of Guanzi, a collection of essays on political science, and a founding father of Legalism.

Hachiman Japanese god of war, referred to as a bodhisattva, or Buddhist saint, from amalgamation of Shinto and Buddhist rites; conceived of as a protective spirit.

Han dynasty (China, 206 B.C.E.–220 C.E.) Broken by the Xin (New) dynasty (9–25 C.E.) into the Former, or Western, Han and the Latter, or Eastern, Han. The Han dynasty stamped its signature on Chinese culture and politics so deeply that this is the origin of the term *Han* now used to refer to the majority ethnic group in China.

Han Fei (ca. 280–233 B.C.E.) A very influential Chinese political philosopher of the Warring States era. He opposed the Mencian idea of the innate goodness of humanity, insisting instead that human nature is evil and therefore requires education, training, and especially law. He is sometimes called a Confucian, sometimes a Legalist, sometimes a Taoist.

Han Xin (d. 196 B.C.E.) A Chinese military strategist and field commander who assisted in the founding of the monumental Han dynasty (206 B.C.E.–220 C.E.). Eventually he was demoted, arrested, and executed on conspiracy charges, as his abilities and influence were regarded as a menace to the state once the Han order was established.

Hayato A contraction of Hayahito, which literally means "swift men," the epithet given the people of a tribe anciently inhabiting Kyushu, the southernmost of the four main islands of Japan. In Japanese history, the Hayato were a military auxiliary drawn from these people, who were subjugated and ultimately annihilated. The Hayato were used for security purposes and as an imperial guard and were also made to perform traditional folk dances at certain formal functions. In ancient times the Hayato were particularly associated with magical warfare, later a specialty of Left-Hand Tantric Buddhists.

Hirate Masahide (1492–1553) A tutor of the Japanese warlord Oda Nobunaga. Hirate committed suicide because of the odd behavior of his ward, the future hegemon, who was still a teenager at the time.

Hojo Nakatoki Chief of the Kyoto agency of the Kamakura Bakufu from 1330 to 1333; he committed suicide in 1333 when Kamakura fell in a civil war.

Hojo Takatoki (1303–1333) Fourteenth-generation regent of the Kamakura Shogunate. When he first assumed this role at the age of fourteen, the real power was held by others. The military government of Japan was so corrupt by this time that the old aristocracy staged a rebellion. When Kamakura was attacked in 1333, the Hojo family committed suicide.

Honda Shigetsugu A vassal of Tokugawa Ieyasu, the founder and first shogun of the Tokugawa era of Japanese history in the early seventeenth century.

Hosokawa Yoriyuki (1329–1392) A successful Japanese military commander, deputy shogun from 1367 to 1379 under Ashikaga rule.

Huang Shi (third century B.C.E.**)** A Chinese military strategist, reputed author of *San Lue*, or *Three Strategies*; alleged to have taught Zhang Liang, would-be assassin of the First Emperor of China. For excerpts from *Three Strategies*, see Thomas Cleary, *Ways of Warriors, Codes of Kings*, 1999.

Imagawa Sadayo (1326–1420) Served under the second Ashikaga shogun; authored *Nan-Taiheiki*, a critique of the historical epic *Taiheiki* treating the period of civil division of the so-called era of the Northern and Southern courts in fourteenth-century Japan.

Jimmu The first emperor of Japan according to Shinto mythology, often mentioned in bushido lore in connection with the so-called Eastern Expedition of Jimmu, referring to an ancient invasion from Kyushu into Honshu, supposedly bringing the heartland of the future Japanese state under the rule of the Yamato emperor.

Kato Kiyomasa (1562–1611) A general under the Japanese hegemon Toyotomi Hideyoshi, he went to Korea for both Hideyoshi and Tokugawa Ieyasu.

Kenshin. See Uesugi Kenshin.

Kublai Khan (1215–1294) A grandson of Genghis Khan, Kublai completed the Mongol conquest of China. He founded the Yuan dynasty, destroyed the remnants of the Song dynasty in southern China, and unified China under Mongolian rule. Kublai also launched two attempts to invade Japan, both unsuccessful but nonetheless destabilizing to the Japanese military government.

Kitabatake Chikafusa (1293–1354) A member of the old Japanese aristocracy and minister of the Southern imperial court during the struggle between Northern and Southern courts in fourteenth-century Japan.

Kitano, deity of Shinto god of disaster, chief deity of thunder demons. Believed to be the avenging spirit of Sugawara Michizane, who was Minister of the Right under Emperor Daigo. Michizane was exiled to Kyushu by the Fujiwara clan in a political struggle and died there in 903.

Koguryo One of the three ancient kingdoms of Korea, founded in 37 B.C.E., independent until 668 C.E.

Koku Equivalent to 5.119 U.S. bushels; a standard unit of dry weight, commonly used to define official salaries (paid in rice) and fief sizes (measured in rice production).

Kongming of Shu. See Zhuge Liang.

Kusunoki Masashige (d. 1336) A great hero of Japanese history. Governor of two provinces, Kusunoki was also a member of several organs of the imperial government under Emperor Go-Daigo, whose legitimacy Kusunoki and his whole family defended during a civil war between rival factions of samurai backing two different imperial courts during the era called Nanboku-cho, or Southern and Northern courts, an anomalous episode in Japanese history. Kusunoki died fighting the warlord Ashikaga Takauji, who was the founder of the second military dynasty, known as Ashikaga after the surname of the Shoguns or as Muromachi after the place of the seat of the government.

Lao Tzu (Laozi) An archetypal Taoist figure, said to have been an archivist of the Zhou dynasty, reputed author of the *Tao Te Ching* (*Daodejing*), a central Taoist classic. See Thomas Cleary, *The Essential Tao*, 1990. A recently discovered pre-Qin version of this text is also translated in Thomas Cleary, *Sex, Health, and Long Life*, 1994.

Liezi (Lieh-tzu) A Chinese literary work attributed to a fourth-century B.C.E. author but in its present form generally ascribed to the third to fourth century C.E., officially designated a Taoist scripture in the eighth century C.E. For extracts, see Thomas Cleary, *Vitality, Energy, Spirit*, 1991.

Li Guang (d. 119 B.C.E.) A famous general of Han dynasty China in its wars against the Huns in the late second century B.C.E. Beloved by his troops but allegedly erratic and controversial, Li committed suicide to avoid court martial after he got lost in a desert campaign and let a Hun chieftain slip away.

Lin Hejing (968–1028) A Chinese poet of the Song dynasty, when unity of Buddhism, Confucianism, and Taoism was made into a major cultural and educational theme.

Li Taibo (1010–1059) A famous Chinese scholar and teacher of the Song dynasty, a professor of classics.

Lu, Master See Lu Donglai.

Luan Cheng An assistant to the lord of an ancient state during China's Spring and Autumn era (eighth to fifth centuries B.C.E.). When his state was attacked and his lord was killed, Luan Cheng was offered a post by the invading lord, but he refused and went to his death fighting the usurpers.

Mr. Lu (Buwei; ca. 291–235 B.C.E.) The prime minister (and reputed illegitimate father) of the First Emperor of China, author of the *Annals of Mr. Lu*.

Lu Xiangshan (1139–1193) A distinguished neo-Confucian philosopher of China. He served in government and was also a teacher and a writer. He is noted for his affinity to Chan Buddhism and emphasized self-examination, influencing the later Wang Yangming.

Maeda Toshiie (1539–1599) A former vassal of the warlord and hegemon Oda Nobunaga who assisted the latter in his drive to unify Japan. Maeda also fought for Oda's successor Toyotomi Hideyoshi, and for the guardian of Hideyoshi's son Hideyori. A student of Zen, Maeda is one of the rare samurai who earned the honor of the *inka*, or seal of approval, testifying to his mastery of Zen.

Maki The battle of Maki took place in 1584, pitting Tokugawa Ieyasu against Toyotomi Hideyoshi, two of the most powerful men in Japanese history, contending for control.

Manners of Zhou Part of the *Classic of Manners*, a Chinese classic detailing the rituals, customs, and courtesies of the upper class of the Zhou dynasty, attributed to the Duke of Zhou, ca. 1100 B.C.E., reconstituted by Confucius ca. 500 B.C.E.

Manyoshu A famous collection of classical Japanese poetry from the seventh and eighth centuries. Containing thousands of poems in Japanese plus some poetry and prose in Chinese, this revered collection is an essential source for Japanese philology.

Masters of Huainan Considered a Taoist classic but also classified as a miscellany, a collection of Chinese lore compiled in the second century B.C.E. For extracts, see Thomas Cleary, *The Book of Leadership and Strategy*, 1991.

Meng Hechun A Confucian scholar of Ming-dynasty China, ca. 1500.

Michiomi-no-Mikoto A Shinto god, ancestral deity of the Mononobe military clan of ancient times.

Mikawa knights Mikawa was the original base of Tokugawa Ieyasu, who was to become the first shogun of the Tokugawa (Edo) period of Japanese history in the beginning of the seventeenth century.

Mimana (Imna) Commonly claimed by Japanese historians to have been an ancient Japanese colony in southern Korea, allegedly established in the late fourth century and maintained for more than two hundred years. This legend was made into a cornerstone of modern Japanese colonial imperialism in Korea. Historians who are not professionally obliged to embrace this line suggest that Imna was really a member of the Kaya federation of southern Korea (42–562 C.E.). Some say the Japanese presence in Imna was an office of diplomacy and trade, not a colony or territory.

Minamoto Yoshitsune (1159–1189) Brother of Yoritomo, founder of the Kamakura Shogunate of Japan. He was allied with his brother in the process of taking over Japan, but after occupying the imperial capital, Kyoto, he became friendly with the emperor. Rejected by his brother the shogun, he rebelled, lost, fled, and was later forced to commit suicide by his protectors, who were of the Fujiwara clan, close allies of the imperial house who were in fear of Yoritomo's wrath.

Mind Studies Shingaku, a lay sociospiritual uplift movement originating in late feudal Japan, combining Zen and neo-Confucianism. Under the laws of the Tokugawa military regime, it was illegal for lay people to teach Buddhism, so this Shingaku movement was founded by lay Zen masters (notably Ishida Baigan and Tejima Toan) to bypass this law and bring practical religion directly to common people outside monastic contexts. The Mind Studies movement still exists, and members are still known to attend Zen lectures and exercises as did the founders.

Ming dynasty China, 1368–1644.

Miyake Takanori (fourteenth century) Also called Kojima Takanori, Bigo Saburo, and so forth, Miyake Takanori was a medieval Japanese warrior said to be descended from the noble Fujiwara clan. Conceiving an ambition to destroy the Hojo clan while still a boy, Miyake fought for the emperor Go-Daigo in the civil war of 1331 and continued to serve the Southern court during the division of the imperial authority into rival northern and southern courts backed by competing samurai factions. He appears in the classic war novel *Taiheiki*, since the Edo period (seventeenth to nineteenth centuries), he has become something of a national hero, considered exemplary for his loyalty to the Southern court.

Miyamoto Musashi (1584–1645) A famous swordsman, an independent samurai, author of the famous *Book of Five Rings*. For

261

Musashi's thought, see Thomas Cleary, *The Japanese Art of War*, 1991, and Thomas Cleary, *The Book of Five Rings*, 1993.

Mononobe An ancient military clan or guild in the service of the early emperors of Japan. See also Mumashimade-no-Mikoto, Nigihayahi-no-Mikoto.

Moritz Benyovszky (1746–1786) A Slovak noble from Hungary who fought for Poland in its war of independence against Russia. Captured by the Russians, Benyovszky was exiled to Siberia. He escaped, then proceeded to explore the Pacific, including the waters surrounding Japan. In 1776 he became king of Madagascar; in 1779 he went to America for support against the English, using Madagascar as a military base. He lost his life fighting on the side of the French against the English in Madagascar.

Mumashimade-no-Mikoto Or, Mumashimaji-no-Mikoto, a Shinto deity who according to Shinto mythology was the leader of the celestial warriors of the Mononobe military clan who assisted the first emperor, Jimmu, in his conquests.

Nagasunehiko A chieftain of the divine age of Japanese prehistory, slain during the so-called Eastern Expedition of the first emperor, Jimmu. Nagasunehiko opposed Jimmu's conquest of the central provinces of the main island but was killed by Nigihayahi-no-Mikoto, another local chieftain, who allied with the invading Jimmu.

Nakatomi no Kamatari (614–669) Forefather of the powerful Fujiwara clan, which dominated gold mining in ancient Japan; traditionally provided brides for emperors and generally held the most powerful posts in the imperial establishment.

Nigihayahi-no-Mikoto A Shinto deity, patron god of the ancient Mononobe warrior guild that helped to establish Yamato rule on the main island of Japan.

Ninigi-no-Mikoto Shinto god of rice, represented in Japanese mythology as a grandson of Amaterasu, the sun goddess.

Nintoku The sixteenth emperor of Yamato, precursor of Japan. Nintoku was the crown prince of the great emperor Ojin, who is believed to have lived in the first half of the fifth century C.E.

Nitta Yoshisada (1301–1338) Nitta supported Emperor Go-Daigo against the Hojo clan, allies of the Minamoto clan, who dominated the Kamakura military government, and against Ashikaga Takauji, who would found the Ashikaga military dynasty in Muromachi.

Oda Nobunaga (1534–1582) A powerful Japanese warlord who virtually unified Japan after the dissolution of the second military dynasty of the Ashikaga Shoguns. Oda was a convert to Christianity and an enemy of Buddhism, particularly infamous for razing thousands of monasteries on Mount Hiei, the stronghold of Tendai Buddhism. His laws also specifically nominate Confucianism as the desired intellectual discipline for samurai serving in government.

Oirats A pastoral people of Central Asian origin. Absorbed into the Mongolian empire in the thirteenth century, the Oirats later emerged as an alliance of four major tribes. At the height of their power, Oirats unified Mongolia and invaded Ming-dynasty China in 1449.

Ojin Fifteenth emperor of Yamato, apotheosized into the Japanese war god Hachiman.

Osasagi, Prince The future emperor Nintoku, q.v.

Qi, Master Qi Gua, a military inspector for the Liang dynasty and military attaché of the Chen dynasty, both short-lived Southern courts of mid-sixth-century China.

Qin dynasty (China, 221–207 B.C.E.) The Qin dynasty first unified China and created the Chinese empire.

Records of Ancient Matters The *Kojiki*, an eighth-century reconstruction of Shinto myth and early Japanese history.

Records of Japan Nihongi, the ancient history of Japan.

Records of Manners The *Li Ji*, along with *Zhou Li* (Manners of Zhou), a Chinese classic supposed to contain records of the culture of the Zhou dynasty (1122–255 B.C.E.); allegedly compiled by Confucius.

Richu The seventeenth emperor of Yamato, first son of Nintoku, who is believed to have lived in the fifth century C.E.

Saito Sanemori (1129–1183) A warrior of the late Heian era, a commander serving the Taira clan, one of the major samurai powers of the time. He died in combat fighting the Minamoto clan during the Genpei War.

Seven virtues of warriors A concept cited from the Chinese classic *Spring and Autumn Annals, Zuo Tradition:* stopping violence, assembling militias, preserving stature, determining merit, securing the populace, harmonizing the masses, increasing wealth.

Silla One of the three ancient kingdoms of Korea, independent from 57 B.C.E. to 935 C.E.

Sima Rangju Chinese strategist, supposed to be the author of *The Warrior Code of the Charioteers.*

Six bandits A Buddhist term for the objects of the six senses in respect to their capacity to "steal" attention.

Six nobles of Jin The patriarchs of six main clans or lineages of the states of Jin during China's Spring and Autumn era.

Song dynasty (China, 960–1278) The Song dynasty was culturally distinguished by the emergence of neo-Confucianism and neo-Taoism under the influence of Chan Buddhism, particularly in terms of the intellectual movement known as the Unity of the Three Teachings (of Confucianism, Taoism, and Buddhism). Politically and militarily the Song was plagued by unstable relations with central and northern Asian neighbors, occasioning internal conflict within the Chinese government surrounding questions of foreign policy.

Sugawara Michizane (845–903) An aristocrat and Confucian scholar of Heian-era Japan, he worked for two emperors, Uda and Daigo, and was appointed ambassador to Tang-dynasty China. Sugawara did not take up the post, and moreover argued successfully for the abolition of cultural missions to China, perhaps because of the decline of the now moribund Tang dynasty. He emphasized Shinto and native Japanese traditions and after his death was apotheosized as the patron deity of scholarship.

Sujin The tenth emperor of Yamato, sometimes conflated with Jimmu, the first emperor of Yamato. Sujin is thought by some to have lived in the third century C.E. but is also considered by some to have lived in the first century B.C.E. According to one tradition, in 88 B.C.E. Sujin sent armies to several regions to attack anyone who didn't submit to his rule, significantly expanding the Yamato sphere of hegemony.

Sun Bin (d. 316 B.C.E.) Also called Sun Tzu, a descendant of the Chinese military scientist Sun Wu, Sun Bin was also a military scientist and author of a manual of war tactics. For a translation of Sun Bin's work, see Thomas Cleary, *The Lost Art of War,* 1996.

Sun Wu (ca. 544–496 B.C.E.) Sun Tzu, one of the most famous military strategists in Chinese history, author of *The Art of War.*

Taigong A Chinese historical hero, Jiang Ziya, an ancient savant and strategist who assisted kings Wen and Wu in establishing the Zhou dynasty in the twelfth century B.C.E. For sayings attributed to Taigong, see selections from *Six Strategies* in Thomas Cleary, *Ways of Warriors, Codes of Kings,* 1999.

Takeda Shingen (1521–1573) A famous warlord of Japan's Warring States era. Deposing his father to take over leadership of his clan in 1541, he solidified his leadership by promotion of public works and industrial enterprise. Turning on his allies, he eventually defeated Oda Nobunaga and Tokugawa Ieyasu, both redoubtable warriors and incomparable figures in Japanese history, but he died before he was able to take advantage of these victories.

Takamikazuchi-no-Mikoto The Shinto thunder god of Kagoshima, traditional guardian of seafaring, was also revered as a god of the sword, god of archery, and god of war. Portrayed as a leader of the military conquest of Japan by the imperial alliance of Yamato, he was probably an apotheosized warrior of prehistoric times. According to Shinto myth, Takamikazuchi-no-Mikoto and Futsunushi-no-Mikoto descended from heaven to convince the earth deity Okuninushi to cede control of Izumo to the celestial deities. Takamikazuchi-no-Mikoto is supposed to have been born from the blood on the sword used by the deity Izanagi to kill the god of fire.

Tang Founder of the Shang dynasty ca. 1766 B.C.E., a hero and model of virtue in Chinese political science. The expression "Tang and Wu" refers to the founders of the Shang and Zhou dynasties as historical heroic figures; their "punitive operations" refer to their overthrow of their predecessors, alleged to be hopelessly corrupt.

Tang dynasty (China, 618–907) The Tang dynasty represents to some scholars the peak of cosmopolitanism in Chinese culture. The development of the imperial government and court culture of Japan was deeply and deliberately influenced by Tang China through cultural missions.

Tenchi, Emperor (626–672) Emperor of Japan, said to have compiled the first Japanese legal code, based on Chinese models. See Wallace Johnson, *The T'ang Code*, 1997.

Third Ashikaga Shogun. See Ashikaga Shogun, Third.

Three evils States of being characterized by the three poisons (q.v.), a Buddhist term for degeneracy.

Three poisons Greed, aggression, and folly; a Buddhist term for basic psychological distortions.

Tian Wenxiang A Chinese civil and military officer of the Song dynasty who worked in both diplomatic and military resistance to the Mongol invasion of China in the thirteenth century. Imprisoned twice by the Mongols, he was finally executed for refusing to work for the conquering khan.

Toyotomi Hideyoshi (1537–1598) One of the most powerful warlords of late medieval Japan, Toyotomi contributed to the unification of Japan following the achievements of Oda Nobunaga.

Having risen from a lowly social status himself, Toyotomi began the process of disarming commoners to reduce the opportunity for others like himself. After his Japanese conquests, Toyotomi launched an invasion of Korea. Opinion of Toyotomi Hideyoshi is mixed, some revering him as a great warrior and conqueror, others dismissing him as a violent and immoral man.

Tradition of Mr. Zuo Traditions of Mr. Zuo on the Spring and Autumn Annals, a Chinese classic purporting to be a chronicle of events during the Spring and Autumn period of preimperial Chinese history, from the eighth to the fifth centuries B.C.E.

Two founders of the Han dynasty The original founder of the Han dynasty in China was Liu Bang (256–195 B.C.E.); the second founder, who revived the Han after a coup d'etat, was Liu Xiu, or Emperor Guangwu, 5 B.C.E.–51 C.E.

Uesugi Kenshin (1530–1578) Uesugi Terutora, a distinguished Japanese warlord of the Warring States era. His rivalry with contemporary Takeda Shingen is legendary. The name Kenshin, by which he is commonly referred, was actually his Buddhist name, taken after his tonsure. A fervent student of Zen, he is reputed to have had a habit of sitting in meditation by night instead of staying with his concubines.

Uji no Wakiiratsuko Half brother of the Yamato emperor Nintoku. Nintoku's tomb is the largest of all the ancient Japanese emperors; he is said to have been the first to embody a (Confucian) ideal of rule by virtue of benevolence to the populace. Uji no Wakiiratsuko is said to have committed suicide to resolve a succession dispute and clear the way for his brother Nintoku (then Prince Osasagi) to assume the throne.

Urabe no Suetake A warrior in the service of Minamoto Yorimitsu (944–1021), a comrade of Watanabe no Tsuna (q.v.), a legendary Japanese military hero whose exploits are framed in mythic terms.

Wako Japanese pirates, a term used for privateers of the middle ages operating out of Shikoku. It has been asserted that Wako groups came to include a considerable percentage of personnel from Korea, and later Portugal as well, though under Japanese command. This theory emphasizes the independence of the Wako from the control of any central government or national body.

Wang Yangming (1472–1529) A Chinese neo-Confucian philosopher, influenced by Lu Xiangshan's advocacy of inner reflection and also by Chan Buddhist contemplative methods. He served the Ming dynasty in both military and civil roles. See J. C. Cleary, *Worldly Wisdom*, 1991.

Warring States era A term for specific periods of history dominated by warfare. In Chinese history, this refers to the period from 480 to 221 B.C.E.; in Japanese history, the period from 1467 to 1573 C.E.

Watanabe no Tsuna (953–1025) A warrior in the service of Minamoto Yorimitsu (944–1021) before the Minamoto clan founded the Kamakura Shogunate. His military feats are shrouded in fabulous legends.

Wei Liaozi A Chinese military classic attributed to the fourth or third century B.C.E., China's Warring States era. For excerpts from this work, see Thomas Cleary, *Ways of Warriors, Codes of Kings*, 1999.

Wei Qing (d. 106 B.C.E.) A Chinese general of the Han dynasty distinguished in Han wars against the Huns.

Wu of Zhou, King Founded the proto-Chinese Zhou dynasty ca. 1122 B.C.E., overthrowing King Zhou of the Shang dynasty

King Wu is a great hero of traditional Chinese history and Confucian ideology.

Wu Tzu's *Art of War* A treatise on military science by Wu Qi (d. 381 B.C.E.), a political reformer and military strategist of China's Warring States era. For selections from this work, see Thomas Cleary, *Ways of Warriors, Codes of Kings*, 1999.

Wu-Yue Spring and Autumn Annals Or, *Annals of Wu and Yue*, compiled about 52 C.E., a collection of materials relating to the history and culture of the Wu and Yue regions of eastern China.

Xia The first historical dynasty of China, traditionally reckoned to have lasted more than four hundred years, from 2205 to 1766 B.C.E. Also used in literature as a general name for China and things Chinese.

Xiang of Chu, King Xiang Jie, a leader of a rebellion against the Qin dynasty, the first Chinese empire, in the late third century B.C.E. He established himself as king of Chu, a large state in the south, but was eventually overcome by Liu Bang, another rebel leader against the Qin, who eventually founded the Han dynasty in 206 B.C.E.

Xiang of Song, Duke A feudal lord of China's Spring and Autumn era, symbolic of ineffectual benevolence. He rallied an alliance of lords and contested the powerful state of Chu for hegemony but lost out in war because of reluctance to use hard tactics on account of his professed idealism based on ancient philosophy, incurring the reproach of his countrymen and ultimately dying of his wounds.

Xun, Master. See Xunzi.

Xun Kuang. See Xunzi.

Xunzi (310–220 B.C.E.) Xun Kuang, one of the most famous Chinese political philosophers of the late Warring States era.

Yagyu Hyogo (1579–1650) Younger brother of Yagyu Munenori, the master swordsman and author of *Family Traditions on the Art of War.* See Thomas Cleary, *The Soul of the Samurai,* 2005.

Yamamoto Kansuke (1501–1561) A famous Japanese military scientist, strategic advisor to the warlord Takeda Shingen.

Yao and Shun Legendary rulers of predynastic China, models of virtue famous for "courteous abdication" to chosen successors in preference to biological successors.

Yellow Emperor A Chinese cultural hero, an ancient ruler traditionally assigned to the mid-third millennium B.C.E. A number of books are attributed to the Yellow Emperor in Taoist tradition. One such work, *The Book of Hidden Correspondences,* is considered a classic of strategic science as well as a guide to self-mastery.

Yuan dynasty China, 1276–1368.

Zeng, Master A senior disciple of Confucius.

Zhang Xun A Chinese military scientist, degree holder, and bureaucrat. He raised an army against the rebellious official An Lushan in 755, holding out for months before finally being overcome and killed when reinforcements were withheld by a would-be rival. He was awarded an honorific posthumous title in recognition of his patriotism.

Zhou The last preimperial dynasty of ancient China, reckoned as existing from the twelfth to the third centuries B.C.E. Zhou culture was held up as an ideal in original Confucianism.

Zhou, King The last ruler of the proto-Chinese Shang dynasty, reigned ca.1154–1122 B.C.E. Notorious for corruption, King Zhou of Shang was deposed by King Wu of the state of Zhou (q.v.). King Zhou is a standard figure of contempt in Chinese lore, normally cited together with King Jie, last ruler of the dynasty before him and similarly symbolic of corruption.

Zhuge. See Zhuge Liang.

Zhuge Kongming. See Zhuge Liang.

Zhuge Liang (181–234) Also referred to by the honorific name Kongming, a great civil and military hero of the kingdom of Shu during the tumultuous Three Kingdoms era of Chinese history (220–265). Zhuge was particularly famous as a strategist, although he is criticized in some circles for having been too humane and therefore too cautious. For readings in his works, see Thomas Cleary, *Mastering the Art of War*, 1989.

Zisi A grandson of Confucius; he studied with Confucius's famous disciple Master Zeng.

BIBLIOGRAPHY

Asayama Ensho, ed. *Rokujo Engi.* Tokyo: Sankibo Busshorin, 1935.

Bi Yuan. *Xu Zizhitongjian.* Shanghai: Shanghai Guji Chubanshe, 1987.

Chen Shou. *San Guo Zhi.* Beijing: Zhonghua Shuju, 1959.

Doi Takeo. *Omote to Ura.* Tokyo: Kobundo, 1985.

Du Yu: *Chunqiujingzhuan Jijie.* Shanghai: Shanghai Guji Chubanshe, 1988.

Fan Shoukang. *Zhongguo Zhexueshi Gangyao.* Taibei: Kaiming Shudian, 1964.

Fan Xuanling, annotator. *Guanzi.* Shanghai: Shanghai Guji Chubanshe, 1987.

Fujimoto Tsuchishige, ed. *Bankei Zenji Hogoshu.* Tokyo: Shunjusha, 1971.

Funai Koyu. *Jinsei Gorin no Sho.* Kyoto: PHP Kenkyusho, 1985.

Gao You, ed. *Zhanguo Ce.* Shanghai: Shanghai Shedian, 1987.

Goto Mitsumura, ed. *Hakuin Osho Zenshu.* Tokyo: Ryuginsha, 1934.

Han Fei: *Han Fei Zi.* Shanghai: Shanghai Guji Chubanshe, 1989.

Ha-u Ho-o [pseud.]. *Gendai Sojizen Hyoron.* Tokyo: Mizuho Shoten, 1970.

Hirano Jinkei. *Nihon no Kamigami.* Tokyo: Kodansha, 1983.

Hong Liangji, ed. *Chunqiu Zuozhuangu.* Beijing: Zhonghua Shuju, 1987.

Hosaka Koji, ed. *Tsurezuregusa.* Tokyo: Gakutosha, n.d.

————, ed. *Koji, Seigo, Kotowaza.* Tokyo: Gakutosha, 1973.

Ikebe Yoshinori: *Nihon Hosei-shi Shomoku Kaidai.* Tokyo: Daitokaku, 1918.

Imamichi Tomonobu. *Bi ni Tsuite.* Tokyo: Kodansha, 1973.

Inoue Tetsujiro, ed. *Bushido Sosho.* Tokyo: Hakubunkan, 1905.

————, ed. *Bushido Shu.* Tokyo: Shunyodo, 1920.

Itasaka Gen. *Nihonjin no Ronri Kozo.* Tokyo: Kodansha, 1991.

Ito Shunko, ed. *Eihei Koroku Chukai Zensho.* Tokyo: Komeisha, 1964.

Jiang Yinxiang, tr. *Shijing Yaozhu.* Beijing: Beijingshi Zhongguoshudian, 1982.

Jiang Yiqing, ed. *Sima Bingfa.* Taibei: Lian-A Chubanshe, 1982.

Jojima Masayoshi, ed. *Hagakure.* Tokyo: Shinjinbutsu-Orai Sha, 1976.

Kabutogi Shoko, ed. *Nichiren Bunshu.* Tokyo: Iwanami Shoten, 1968.

Kanatani Osamu, tr. *Lunyu.* Tokyo: Iwanami Shoten, 1963.

————, tr. *Sunzi.* Tokyo: Iwanami Shoten, 1963.

————, tr. *Zhuangzi.* Tokyo: Iwanami Shoten, 1983.

Kawasaki Yasuyuki, et al., eds. *Shukyoshi.* Tokyo: Sansen Shuppansha, 1965.

Kiriyama Yasuo. *Nenriki.* Tokyo: Tokuma Shoten, 1975.

Kobayashi Katsundo, tr. *Mengzi.* Tokyo: Iwanami Shoten, 1972.

Koda Rentaro, ed. *Shido Bunan Zenji Shu.* Tokyo: Shunjusha, 1956.

Kong Yingda, annotator. *Shangshu Zhengyi.* Taibei: Zhonghua Shudian, 1977.

Kubota Jun, ed. *Myoe Shonin Shu.* Tokyo: Iwanami Shoten, 1981.

Kusumoto Bunyu. *Sodai Jugaku no Zen Shiso Kenkyu.* Nagoya, Japan: Nisshindo Shoten, 1980.

Li Jiemin, tr. *Weiliaozi Yaozhu.* Beijing: Hebei Renmin Chubanshe, 1992.

Li Jiurui. *Xianqin Shizi Sixiang Gaishu*. Taibai: Taibei Shudian, 1972.

Li Ling. *Simafa Yaozhu*. Shijiazhuang: Hebei People's Press, 1992.

Li Zhi. *Zangshu*. Taibei: Xuesheng Shuju, 1974.

Liu Ji. *Baizhan Qilue*. Beijing: Guangming Ribao Chubanshe, 1987.

Lu Zhan. *Song Sizi Shaoyao*. Taibei: Shijie Shuju, 1972.

Matsushita Konosuke. *Jissen Keiei Tetsugaku*. Kyoto: PHP Kenkyusho, 1978.

————. *Keiei Kokorecho*. Kyoto: PHP Kenkyusho, 1974.

Mizunoue Tsutomu. *Ikkyu*. Tokyo: Chuokoronsha, 1978.

Mori Keizo, ed. *Kinsei Zenrin Genkoroku*. Tokyo: Nihon Tosho Senta, 1977.

Mori Senzo, ed. *Kinsei Kijin Den*. Tokyo: Iwanami Shoten, 1940.

Morita Shoma. *Meishin to Mozo*. Tokyo: Hakuyosha, 1983.

Muji Zenji. *Shasekishu*. Kyoto: Heiryakuji Shoten, 1933.

Nakahara Toju. *Nantenbo Angyaroku*. Tokyo: Hirakawa Shuppansha, 1984.

Nukariya Kaiten. *Wakan Meishi Sanzen Shu*. Tokyo: Shueisha, 1915.

Obashi Shunyu, ed. *Ippen Shonin Goroku*. Tokyo: Iwanami Shoten, 1985.

Odaka Kunio. *Nihonteki Keiei*. Kyoto: Chuokoronsha, 1984.

Ogawa Tamaki, et al., trs. *Shiki Retsuden*. Tokyo: Iwanami Shoten, 1975.

Ogiya Shozo. *Gendai Bijinesu Kingenshu*. Kyoto: PHP Kenkyusho, 1986.

Ogura Masahiko. *Chugoku Kodai Seiji Shiso Kenkyu*. Tokyo: Aoki Shoten, 1970.

Omori Sogen. *Ken to Zen*. Tokyo: Shunjusha, 1983.

Qiang Yiqing, ed. *Sima Bingfa.* Taibei: Lian-A Chubanshe, 1981.

Sahashi Horyu. *Ningen Keizan.* Tokyo: Shunjusha, 1979.

Sakurai Yoshiro. *Chusei Nihon no Oken, Shukyo, Geino.* Kyoto: Jinbun Shoin, 1988.

Sato Taishun, ed. *Muchu Mondo.* Tokyo, Iwanami Shoten, 1935.

Sekiguchi Shindai, tr. *Makashikan.* Tokyo: Iwanami Shoten, 1966.

Shibata Renzaburo. *Nemuri Kyoshiro Mujo Hikae.* Tokyo: Shunjusha, 1981.

Sueki Takehiro. *Toyo no Gori Shiso.* Tokyo: Kodansha, 1970.

Suzuki Daisetsu. *Imakita Kosen.* Tokyo: Shunjusha, 1975.

Suzuki Tesshin, ed. *Suzuki Shosan Dojin Zenshu.* Tokyo: Sankibo Busshorin, 1962.

Takahashi Junichi, ed. *Heike Monogatari.* Tokyo: Kodansha, 1972.

Takeda Shinji, tr. *Yijing.* Tokyo: Iwanami Shoten, 1969.

Takuan Zenji. *Roshi Kowa.* Tokyo: To-A-Do Shobo, 1910.

Tiannan Yisou [pseud.]. *Zhouyi Qigong.* Changchun, China: Changchun Chubanshe, 1990.

Tsukamoto Zenryu, ed. *Sekai no Rekishi.* Vol. 4, *To to Indo.* Tokyo: Chuokoronsha, 1975.

Ueyama Shunbei, et al. *Mikkyo no Sekai.* Osaka: Osaka Shoseki, 1982.

Wang Yi, ed. *Huang Di Yinfujing Quanshu.* Xi'an, China: Xiaxi Liuyun Chubanshe, 1992.

Watsuji Tetsuro, ed. *Shobogenzo Zuimonki.* Tokyo: Iwanami Shoten, 1929.

Wei Xing, et al., eds. *Rujia Zhenyanlu.* Huhhot: Inner Mongolia People's Press, 1997.

Yamada Kodo, ed. *Zenmon Hogoshu*. Tokyo: Koyukan, 1895.

Yamazaki Ichisada, ed. *Sekai no Rekishi*. Vol. 6, *So to Gen*. Tokyo: Chuokoronsha, 1976.

Books by Thomas Cleary

The Book of Five Rings, by Miyamoto Musashi
Here is one of the most insightful texts on the subtle arts of confrontation and victory to emerge from Asian culture. Written not only for martial artists but for leaders in all professions, the book analyzes the process of struggle and mastery over conflict that underlies every level of human interaction.

The Book of Leadership and Strategy: Lessons of the Chinese Masters
The subtle arts of management and leadership have been developed over thousands of years by the Chinese. Collected here are insightful teachings on the challenges of leadership on all levels, from organizational management to political statecraft.

The Japanese Art of War: Understanding the Culture of Strategy
Military rule and the martial tradition of the samurai dominated Japanese culture for more than eight hundred years. Citing original Japanese sources that are popular among Japanese readers today, Cleary reveals the hidden forces behind Japanese attitudes and conduct in political, business, social, and personal life.

Mastering the Art of War, by Liu Ji and Zhuge Liang
Composed by two prominent statesmen-generals of classical China, this book develops the strategies of Sun Tzu's classic, *The Art of War*, into a complete handbook of organization and leadership.

Ways of Warriors, Codes of Kings: Lessons in Leadership from the Chinese Classics
Here is a concise and user-friendly presentation of the ancient Chinese principles of leadership and strategy in the words of the masters themselves. Cleary has put together this collection of gems of wisdom from six of the great classics, including excerpts from his best-selling translation of *The Art of War* and other lesser-known but insightful texts.

Zen Lessons: The Art of Leadership
This guide to enlightened conduct for people in positions of authority is based on the teachings of several great Chinese Zen masters. It serves as a guide to recognizing the qualities of a genuine Zen teacher; it also serves as a study of the character and conduct necessary for the mastery of any position of power and authority—whether religious, social, political, or organizational.